A-Z of School Leadership: A guide for new school leaders

Kausor Amin-Ali
BEng (Hons.) MA PGCE (Cantab) NPQH NPQEL FRSA

First published 2021

Independently Published.

Copyright © 2021 Kausor Amin-Ali

Cover design by Rooful Ali; racreation.com

All rights reserved.

No part of this publication may be reprinted, reproduced, utilised or transmitted in any form or by any means, electronic, mechanical, now known or hereafter invented including photocopying, recording, or otherwise, or in any information storage or retrieval system, without prior permission from the publishers.

Opinions expressed in this publication are those of the contributors and are not necessarily those of the publisher. We cannot accept any responsibility for errors or omissions.

The author and publisher does not have any control, or responsibility for, any third-party websites referred to in this book. All internet addresses given in this book were correct at the time of going to press. The author and publisher regret any inconvenience caused if any of the internet addresses have changed or ceased to exist but can accept no responsibility for any such changes.

ISBN: 9798735916024

To all those negative teachers, who (almost) ruined the life chances of hundreds of children:

"Hey! Teacher! Leave them kids alone!"[1]

Dedication

To my wife, Nahida, who has shown tremendous patience in nearly two decades of marriage throughout my absence of many days and nights due to leadership training programmes as well helping me out in my many workload challenges such as washing (and ironing!) the school football team's kit (as we had a fixture backlog playing two games on consecutive days)!

To our young son AbdUllah, who often waited for me to return from work, only to find our planned play activity cancelled as I arrived home too late. Sorry, my son!

Lastly, to all the children of the world . . . who dream, believe and can achieve, if afforded the opportunities built upon equity and social justice. Education is indeed the Golden Ticket.[2] This book is for you.

Contents

Acknowledgements 13
Preface 23
A 27
   Authenticity 27
   Agenda 28
   Accountability 30
B 33
   Blind ambition 33
   Building 36
   Budget 37
C 41
   Change 41
   Context 43
   Collaborate 45
D 47
   Deadlines 47
   Data literate 49
   Delegation 51
E 53
   Equity 53
   E-mail 54
   Envy 56
F 59
   Feedback 59
   Friends 61

Contents

    Fitness 63
G 67
    Generosity 67
    Growth 69
    Governors 71
H 75
    Humility 75
    Hypocrisy 77
    Humour 79
I 81
    Inspection 81
    Interview 84
    Intelligence 87
J 91
    Justice 91
    Juggle 93
    Joy 96
K 99
    Kettle 99
    Kind 100
    Keep 102
L 105
    Listen 105
    Learning outcomes 107
    Legacy 108
M 111
    Meeting 111

Contents

    Membership 113

    Mindfulness 114

N 117

    No 117

    Navigate 119

    Need 120

O 123

    Opportunity 123

    Outstanding 124

    Outliers 126

P 129

    People 129

    Presentations 130

    Pressure 132

Q 135

    Quality Assurance 135

    Question 138

    Qualifications 139

R 143

    Routines 143

    Research 144

    Referee 147

S 149

    Solution 149

    Spheres of influence 150

    School 153

T 155

Contents

- Thought leadership 155
- Technology 156
- Time management 158

U 161
- Understanding 161
- Umbrella 162
- Undertaking 163

V 165
- Vocal 165
- Vehicle 166
- Verbal reasoning 167

W 171
- Work-life balance 171
- Why? 173
- Wins 175

X 177
- X-ray vision 177
- Exception 179
- Axe to grind 180

Y 183
- Yes people 183
- Youthful 185
- Yesterday 186

Z 189
- Zeal 189
- Zone 190
- Zenith 192

Contents

Conclusion..195
About the author 197

Acknowledgements

I begin my acknowledgments in a rather unconventional way compared to all other published books as a narrative of the journey I have had as a child in school and then joining the teaching profession and journeying to school leadership. It is a timeline of my life and career to date as such and acknowledgements are needed along the way to give credit to all those who helped, inspired and supported me.

Firstly, to all the thousands of children/students I have had the privilege to teach, supervise, mentor (and provide references for) and all those whom I have had the chance to help indirectly (by way of managing staff who taught the students,) "thank you" for making this such a worthwhile profession to be part of and adding value to your lives.

Secondly, to all the teachers, colleagues, mentors, peers and friends who inspired me to become a teacher and progress in my career, there are hundreds I could mention, too many to mention; but I will recall some in detail as credit and a personal and professional "thank you" to be given to those who shaped my journey, my thinking and who I am to date. (Conversely, without any bitterness, a big 'no thank you' to all those I have encountered in schools, who derailed the careers of many for their selfish gain and abuse of power who shall remain unnamed and in doing so damaged the life chances of many children.)

In my childhood and adolescence, my sincere thanks to my older brother Rooful and my younger brother Lutfur, who have always supported my career, albeit with a healthy distraction of discussing all things football! To my sister, Panna and of course my parents, whom despite us growing in severe poverty in the 1970s, 1980s and 1990s Britain, always encouraged me to study, work hard and be honest.

Commencing with my Primary School education at All Saints Primary, in Wellingborough: Headteacher Miss Lofthouse; Top Juniors teacher (now known as Year 6) Mrs Watson; and Rev. Haydn Smart whose assemblies remain impactful to this day in 'carrying a burden' and vividly illustrating servant leadership by helping and caring for others as a good Samaritan.

Onto Secondary education and at Wrenn School also in Wellingborough: My Form Tutors: Dr Holmes (Chemistry teacher) whose intellectual brilliance kept me in awe of him; and he was very tall too, so I literally had to look up to him! Mr Whiteley, (Union representative and my IT teacher) whose insight into the politics of education really opened my eyes, but also his playing (on vinyl record in the summer of 1993) Pink Floyd's *'Another Brick in the Wall Pt.2,'* at the end of Fifth Form (Year 11) to remind us that we are not merely bricks in the wall, but individuals in our own right who can go on to achieve. Mrs Stewart in Sixth Form, whose interest in business allowed me to gain a foothold into Project Management and gave me confidence to present in front of audiences.

My Senior Teachers: Mr Walker; Mr Armstrong and Mr Arnold and my Year Leader Mrs Petty. My English teacher: Mr Mulcahy whose 'Booster' 'praise slip' really did give me the boost I needed and instilled a firm belief, with encouragement, I could achieve very well early in secondary school. My Art teacher: Mr Menhinick who also showed an insight into how the world works. My Mathematics teachers: Mr Goodman for the old Grammar school methods (of chalk and do not dare to talk!) and Mr Hagar for the ease of accelerated entry despite my doubts. One of my Science teachers: Mr Wilson who made science so interesting and purposeful. My Geography teacher: Miss Weatherson whose real-life analysis of human impact on the physical world around us has remained with me ever since.

As I completed my Secondary School in Sixth Form, the Head of Sixth Form: Mr MacDougall where you had to earn your stripes to join the ranks of Sixth Form, having been in fear of being shouted at for walking on the wrong side of the corridor and whose ever presence was a bit like Strickland from the movie *'Back to the Future'* i.e. he has been in the school for decades with the same bald head. (Did he ever have hair?!)

Finally at school, my PE teachers Mr Dabbs and Mr Petty who was also

Acknowledgements

my older brother's Form Tutor. The fear of being caught out by their crushing sarcasm (or wit as Mr Petty would put it) and their respect and belief in all the students being able to achieve something in PE. Had Mr Petty not encouraged my older brother to be the first in our household to go to university (and thus breaking down the education poverty cycle in our household), I certainly would not be here now writing this book. Thank you Mr Petty!

At the University of Sheffield, Dr Martin Pitt for his discussions and dialogue on all things plausible and otherwise.

Upon graduating my sincere thanks to Muhammad Houghton, who inspired me and mentored me to embark on a PGCE and become a teacher and apply to the University of Cambridge. Dr (now Prof.) Paul Andrews for giving me the opportunity to train as a teacher and commence my PGCE, despite an incredibly nervous interview!

As a trainee teacher: At Redwell Primary in Wellingborough, Robyn Pickles whose warmth and kindness to children really showed me why education matters. At Ernulf in St Neots, where Dirk Pereira defined the purpose of being a teacher and has a deep and lasting impact on the human element of being a teacher and helping children above all, to feel safe and happy.

At Sharnbrook Upper School in Bedfordshire; Robin Piggott and Cath Carré for their immense support and patience as a trainee Maths teacher. Also, Marion Greaves whose support after my university formal observation was immense as some Year 10 students 'played up' by asking me "what is a graph? What are coordinates? What is x and y?" and I froze in panic and nearly became distraught in front of the class! Peter Rattu for giving me a chance to lead an assembly in Year 10 whilst on my PGCE placement.

Howard Reid, a senior leader at Sharnbrook, having previously taught my sister and both of my brothers at Wrenn School more than 10 years ago. This taught me that working in schools is indeed a small world! Finally, the Principal, Peter Barnard, for not ejecting me from the whole staff meeting, where in my enthusiasm (also known as naïveté) as a PGCE student, I had the audacity to challenge the school management during a whole staff meeting to ask if vertical tutoring is a choice or had it already been agreed by SLT (implying the consultation was a cynical stakeholder engagement ploy)!

Now commencing my career as a 'qualified teacher' of mathematics and as a less qualified form tutor, I owe a lot of thanks to all the staff at Wisewood Secondary School in Sheffield. In particular to my first two line managers: Alida Allen (curriculum) and Janicen Lambeth (pastoral).

As a teacher of mathematics: Alida Allen epitomised dedication in ensuring excellence in her curriculum and department leadership. Her passion for teaching mathematics in a way to engage learners was a true privilege for me to have witnessed for seven years. It led her to 'build' two 'outstanding' departments in succession with Christina Doughty and I as the only remaining members in both 'teams'. Alida is an amazing leader who was able to rebuild time and again while maintaining outstanding outcomes for the students for decades. (I compare this to the great football managers who can assemble and rebuild squads successfully). Other colleagues I owe credit to helping me develop include Jayne Revill, Alan Reay and after their departure, Mick Walton, Kath Green and Toyin Awobajo.

In enabling me to genuinely fulfil 'in loco parentis' as a committed form tutor, I owe a lot to Janicen Lambeth and her efficiency in resolving issues with the much needed 'tough love' when circumstances dictated. My thanks and respect to Sophie Larder, my colleague in the year group as we spent 5 years as form tutors and competing for wins on Sports Days in our inter-form rivalry! Also thanks to Beryl Harlow whose blunt no-nonsense approach in dealing with challenges from unsupportive parents or non-cooperative students was unparalleled and really shaped my future pastoral work.

In my enthusiasm for extra-curricular activities, my sincere thanks to Eric Davis and James Turnbull. I also extend a true appreciation for all

Acknowledgements

those who attended training and the few who were fortunate to have been chosen to be in the school football team. As a coach I acknowledge the players and parents who shared the joy and disappointment (and transport) as we battled the elements and playing much larger schools, always as the underdog, yet winning the occasional cup along the way!

Also, my thanks to Neil Whitehouse and Thom James in IT support and Mal, Les, Mark and Andy as site staff whose patience in my frequent onsite late stay backs after school was deeply appreciated as they did not lock me in the school building!

Also, Khalid Tabani, who as a Student Learning Mentor, helped me tremendously when I was an NQT. His help with that Year 9 class last period on a Tuesday and Wednesday where students walked in and out as they chose to and I felt unable to teach a lesson at times due to the challenges and even considered quitting in the first year of teaching. His support was more over and above. Julie Bloor for supporting me in obtaining three internal promotions in my first five years of teaching. Also, Derek Green, whose professional association support proved to be very helpful in enabling my rights in the teaching profession.

Whilst on Fasttrack; Dr Jeff Jones who gave the most important induction into school leadership training emphasising emotional intelligence as a school leader. Nick Austin and Richard Churches for their purposeful words in all their sessions; Ted Kennedy whose wisdom and support has been immense.

On the Equal Access to Promotion Cohort 5B, Marva Rollins and her life story of leadership and the challenges of racism. Moving and inspiring at the same time and how I ended up being one of the publicity photos for the National College NPQH Gateway Portal!

On Diverse Leaders; Rosemary Campbell-Stephens for broadening my mind on the need for equity and social justice and the facilitation by Baljit Birring and meeting Mohammed Lone with his wisdom, common sense and conviction.

Peter Crowe at Tibshelf, Derbyshire as I sought my next steps of leadership development and later at Shirebrook, Julie Bloor (previously Head at Wisewood) for supporting me with my first promotions in school.

As a Senior Leader at Balby Carr Community College, Doncaster: Martin Craig, Headteacher and mentor, who epitomised the meaning of a 'community' school and reminded me of why we are in education: to improve children's life chances; but also showing me there is a life after Headship and happily enjoying retirement! He also pointed out the importance to be a leader of the future, rather than focus on the future of the leader.

To Paul Kent, Jon Findlay and Marie Coffield for putting students first in face of the battle for academisation, whilst others put their careers first over the students. The team at the Satellite School led by Amanda Taylor who proved that all students could remain in the same school until completion of their education and the team at EdLounge who have supported disadvantaged students for years.

During my time at Future Leaders: Heath Monk and Iain Hall whose 'education is civil rights' presentation brings so much emotion to me to this day and my mentors Ian Cox and Kevin Moloney. Also, during my intervisitation to New York and New Jersey, the community of North Star Academy Charter School in New Jersey and their Principal, Jesse Rector for exemplifying his drive and commitment to ensure every child succeeds no matter what.

To Sonia Parnell for her 'fierce' media training during which sweat never poured so much from me in fear of her tough questioning and grilling! Also, my first attempt to impart wisdom gained during the early days of school leadership as a Leadership Peer Mentor of the East Midlands Cohort 2014, Dr Craig Avieson, Emma Booth, Emma Howard, Andrea Jackson, Nathan Oxford and Adrian Rollins.

At Kings Science Academy in Bradford, Sana Ahmed for her commitment to the students and doing the same motorway journey as

Acknowledgements

me for many months. At Rainbow School, Mohammed Ayub Ismail on how he showed tremendous dignity in matters whilst facing great adversity.

At the University of Nottingham, Prof. Howard Stevenson in shaping my academic writing and influencing my thinking on social mobility matters in school leadership.

In Abu Dhabi, my thanks to Patrick Horne, who in my first sixth months overseas provided me with great support in those turbulent days of relocating from Britain. In Dubai, whilst I was a Principal and Executive Headteacher, the professional friendships and support from fellow Principals and School Leaders namely Mark Steed, Samantha Steed, Michael Lambert, Naveed Iqbal and Karim Murcia and Julian Pederick, but in particular Andrew Gibbs who provided me with an opportunity in the moments of the 'lows' of school leadership.

Innovator Priya Lakhani and the pioneer Javier Arguello for challenging the status quo and education establishment and how they both push the boundaries of what possibilities exist in AI (at Century Tech) and neuroscience (at COGx), respectively.

My thanks to all at Ranches Primary School, "the closest thing to a Finnish school in Dubai" as said in front of the Finnish Ambassador in 2019 during the Finnish Education Expo. A school where I am proud my son attends. This Finnish vision of child-led learning and learning through play under the leadership of Principal Samantha Steed and followed up so smoothly by Julian Pederick and Tom Collar. An example of great succession planning if there ever was.

A vision I also benefitted from was the support that Saara Värtö affirmed in me and my team that I was able to implement and witness a total child-led learning in Year 1, across the curriculum. This gave me hope and confidence in breaking the shackles of dogmatic education where 5-year-olds have daily spelling tests and cursive handwriting practice. Paul Crossley for his great insight and support on all things with technology, innovation and helping me shape the #futureschool dialogue.

Also, an appreciation for my former colleagues in Dubai, Lorraine Fleming, Amanda Wilding, Anisa Haji, Mark Santos, Melanie Pascua and especially Sabitha Varghese and Karen Fugoso whose ability to take on exceptional workloads and multitask was remarkable.

At UCL, Dr. Farid Panjwani, for initiating my first ever publication: a chapter in the series 'Education in the Arab World' edited by Colin Brock and Serra Kirdar. Kim Leatham for her support during my NPQEL studies and my excellent executive leadership coach, Joanne Lally.

Dan Worth at TES, whose support in publishing my first articles, gave me the belief to write about educational matters to the wider community beyond 'my school' gates.

At the University of Birmingham Dubai, Sanam Yaqub and Prof. Colin Diamond in enabling allow me to help bridge the gap and establish the much-needed partnerships of primary, secondary and tertiary education.

Within every school I have worked in or had the privilege to visit, a massive "thank you" to the dozens of cleaners, IT staff, catering staff and maintenance teams (known as 'caretakers' in my era) without whom a school really could not function. Many are a familiar face, but I regret not spending enough time to ask for their names, who they are and learn about their life stories.

I also acknowledge the staff I have led, managed and supported in some way. I hope I have inspired in my time in Yorkshire and Dubai. I learned so much from all of you as well. And the people I have never met but inspired me immensely: Ken Robinson and John West-Burnham.

Outside of 'education' David Casey whose no-nonsense project management made me as sharp and cynical in equal measure but

Acknowledgements

driven for results and task completion at 3663. Steve Edmonds, former National Partner at Grant Thornton LLP, whose corporate career progression showed that you can make it to the very top, but still have empathy and show dignity for new trainees entering the profession. A lesson I carried forward into Headship, from the outset, to meet and get to know trainee and newly qualified teachers.

Penultimately, to my peer reviewers and proof-readers, Muhammad Houghton, Martin Craig, Lutfur Ali, Richard Petty, Andrew Gibbs and Iftikhar Ali.

Lastly, to my personal friends, many prefer not to be named, who have added great value and support in my life. Shazad Butt from a peer at the University of Sheffield to becoming a mathematics teacher has some parallels to my own journey. Ashfaq Khan whose commitment to helping disadvantaged communities and champion social mobility through education in Sheffield is inspiring. Also, my two civil engineer friends, Riyaz Kazi and Guled Hersi, whose journey as engineering graduates from the University of Sheffield to Dubai draws on a route I have taken.

As you can see, it may take a village, to raise a child,[3] but **it takes hundreds of colleagues and thousands of students to raise a school leader.**

Preface

I hope you, the reader, (teachers, educators and school leaders) will benefit from this book in helping to contribute to fulfil the hopes of the children, meet the aspirations of the parents and in doing so realise your own professional ambitions. This book is for all aspiring and current school leaders who want to make a difference to all students in their supervision.

The aim of this book is to set out some key elements of school leadership advice which I gathered along the way in nearly twenty years of education. From the outset, A-Z can oversimplify matters and I have tried to move away from the obvious ones: A: Assessment, P: Parents, T: Teaching to name but three. Invariably there are so many other examples one could have chosen, but I have limited it to three per letter with some editorial privilege for words starting with less used characters in the alphabet!

I 'fell' into teaching after volunteering as a tutor in west London in 2001. From the outset of my PGCE a year later and onwards, I have been fortunate to have had some truly inspirational leaders, whom I have met or even been privileged to have worked with. I have also had some great mentoring and coaching along the way to enable me to reflect as a human being first and foremost and then in the context of education: as a teacher and a school leader.

However, I have also come across the corrupt, devious, self-serving school leaders who talked a good talk and timed their career steps to perfection regardless of what damage was caused along the way. By my very interaction with such school leaders, I learned how NOT to be a school leader like them and how NOT to adopt their selfish mindset and how NOT to be so 'full of yourself' in arrogance, underlined with insecurity.

Experience or as some call it 'on the job training' is valid in the context of a school and, though increasingly rarely, you will encounter a 'one-school teacher' akin to a 'one-club footballer'. With this analogy, I can draw some parallels from professional football management into school leadership.

Once you become a Principal or Headteacher, everybody it seems, has an opinion on how the school should improve and point the finger of blame, rather than the hand of support is surrounding the incumbent. Or another analogy, having climbed the mountain and planted the flag that you expect others to aspire to, it is the fall from the 'top' that has the bigger legacy rather than the journey you have taken the school to have reached the summit in the first instance.

I have broken this down into three examples of each 'letter' but of course one could find a dozen examples in each category. I have deliberately focused on the role of the leader and how their actions impact colleagues and more importantly the student body.

The risk of forgetting where you came from is very real. So many leaders seem to forget what it was like with the hardship and struggle from the outside looking in, or looking up, but once in their (upstairs office) they seem to have the comfort of looking out and looking down.

The leadership deficiency has enabled hundreds of incompetent school leaders to damage schools and ruin children's life chances. It has led to a system of nepotism and corruption (or did nepotism and corruption cause the leadership deficiency?) Schools need great leaders: Individuals committed to the cause of ensuring every school is a safe, happy and successful place for all children learning and for all adults working.

As teachers, we use many acronyms and abbreviations . . . I have tried to explain in parentheses what each one means . . . I start with this one: Welcome to the SLT (Senior Leadership Team)! School leadership is something utterly unique that I have not come across in any other sectors and I have met and discussed with partners of law and accountancy firms, medical consultants and senior managers in business.

The depth and breadth of the responsibility of a school leader is so vast

Preface

that it never seems to end. With a project for example, the completion is clear with milestones of progress along the way. Or with a process, it is very linear and clear for all what is expected in terms of input and output. For example, audit a firm and publish the accounts.

It could be argued, schools have exam results as their 'annual accounts,' but there are so many other factors affecting the student performance and not only the quality of teaching and how well they perform in the exam.

For example, the wellbeing of the student, the family circumstances and welfare issues, psychological factors, friendships and social issues. Many of these are beyond the direct influence of school staff, but they all contribute to the preparation of the student for the exams or qualifications. So, despite the input of teaching and the output of learning, these other non-linear factors can railroad the output usually to the detriment. Other times they can enhance the learning output by way of private tutoring, but this provides unequal opportunities and disadvantages for many unable to bear this additional financial burden.

In addition, the inspection ratings of schools form a perception for all stakeholders based on a judgement of a team of inspectors in a short timeframe. The public or open scrutiny is only on par with football management, but you seldom have a weekly press conference to put the record straight or correct any inaccurate rumours or quell conjecture about what is or is not happening in your school. For example, nobody in the public would even know who oversees a hospital or dare to say if this is a bad hospital or if this is a badly built bridge by just looking at the civil engineers building it, yet people are too quick to label a school as "bad".

Staying with the football theme, the great footballer does not always make a great manager. This is not to say that 'outstanding' teachers cannot be 'outstanding' school leaders. If you are naturally talented, you may not realise what it takes to improve, if you have had limited experience, insight or understanding into requiring improvement or further development, which makes it difficult to coach or mentor or even lead.

Often school leaders who have been consistently outstanding in their teaching career 'counter' this by having team members in SLT who may have been 'good' or 'very good' teachers with occasional 'outstanding' but have working knowledge and insight of improvement and betterment in reaching optimum performance.

The accountability is immense. You can search for 'good schools' but inspections of other (public) services are not quite in the same manner. Imagine a directory to search for civil engineering firms, who have built our roads and comparing their performance. Which firms were more successful in building on time, to a high standard and within budget? Or comparing a 'league table' of dentists and their 'performance' or having inspection ratings of 'outstanding' law firms and their 'success rate'.

Yet, schools do need to be held to account as schools are responsible for the future of a nation. A good school system, well-funded, well-managed by all stakeholders will provide an opportunity for all and build the foundations of an equitable society underpinned with social justice.

A

Authenticity

A lot of leaders 'talk the talk' but their 'A' is ambition (for themselves) and the more they can delegate and take the credit for other colleagues' success, the quicker they can progress in their blinding ambition to their next role. (Refer to Chapter B.) By being authentic, it is not an easy pathway. Your leadership journey in a school may take a lot longer than others, but the roots you plant will be flourishing for years ahead. The best way to remain authentic is simply to always 'be yourself'.

"The world is but a stage and we are actors" is the biggest fallacy sold to many leaders on training courses across many sectors not only in educational leadership. It supports duplicity and role playing and paves the way for a career trajectory built on hypocrisy. (Refer to Chapter H.) You should not be 'faking it' or having to always mask your true feelings or intent. This may sound very self-righteous, but the essence of being in education and working in schools is to encourage children and students to be honest and play by the rules and not to cheat or lie. Yet if the gatekeepers are anything other than this, it is wholly unacceptable.

As a leader, you are expected to take on the role of being 'professional' despite any challenges in your personal life. This does not mean you should divulge your personal issues in the workplace, nor become emotional in school or when representing the school elsewhere.

However, just as schools understand that the personal life(style) can adversely affect the performance and outcomes of students (and the more effective schools engage with dysfunctional households earlier to provide the much-needed support and structure); as a leader, you need to be aware that challenges staff have in their personal settings will no doubt affect their performance in school as it would your own performance. The more effective school leaders show greater empathy in supporting colleagues.

The challenge leaders face is to ensure any personal context is not used for excuses of underperformance, but rather as a possible reason. Overcoming or managing the issue with the intention to address any shortfall in school i.e. making up lost learning time shows the sincerity in a colleague and is one way to identify the genuine reasons rather than the colleague lamenting excuses for being behind in lesson planning or content coverage with a particular class.

To lead by example with an authentic manner, leaders should always look in the mirror. The senior manager is the one standing in front of the mirror, the senior leader is the reflection in the mirror of how the person is viewed by others. If there is any doubt or self-denial of being genuine, reflect and amend this shortcoming.

Agenda

Consider what is the aim or objective of a meeting? What is the purpose of having an item on the agenda? Is it for self-affirmation? Is it to rubber stamp something? Is it to discuss, debate and see pros and cons of a proposed initiative?

Agendas tend to be sent out formally via e-mail (long gone are the paper copies in the pigeonhole!) and with short notice for attendees to prepare! They are literally sent on the day of the meeting or at 8pm or later into the night, the day before. Furthermore, the agenda tends to be e-mailed with several detailed attachments, that you are expected to have read and, in some cases, prepared a response for.

As for duplication, hard copies (pre-COVID) were made available in the meeting with colourful data sheets and charts printed on A3 paper with a few spare copies floating around (with the SLT member queue-jumping in reprographics to have these pages "printed urgently")! Even more frustratingly, the presentation is e-mailed before the meeting, but then presented again verbatim in front of the live attendees which is a rather inefficient use of time; or if active note taking during the presentation, the presenter confirms it will be e-mailed after the presentation. Consider real time presentation sharing as more useful?

If you are the one setting the agenda, look at what needs to be discussed in the meeting. It is always worth having some preparation prior to the meeting for all attendees to enable active participation. Agenda items should not be a simple 'does everyone agree?' topic. If the agenda item does not encourage new thinking, a response or even disagreement from others in the SLT or the staff team then was it worth adding to the agenda for mere endorsement purposes only?

Before setting an agenda, decide who needs to attend and spare the FOMO (Fear of Missing out) mindset, that it ought to be a multi-person meeting with the whole of SLT or the whole faculty which brings with it the risk of obvious challenge of tardiness by way of increased attendees. Also, consider how much time is expected for each agenda item to be discussed and the expected outcome. Remember the SLT meeting is the costliest regular meeting in the whole school, with the highest earners in attendance, therefore do ensure value for money and quality input and output. ('All staff' or 'whole school' meetings are by default the costliest meetings and need careful planning for what is expected to be presented. Refer to Chapter P.)

If you are expected to contribute to the agenda rather than lead or chair the meeting, ensure it is relevant for others. Of course, it is relevant to you, by default, but who else needs to be informed and what input do you need from others? I have sat in many meetings discussing student attainment or quality of teaching and learning and the other members of SLT who are not directly associated with it are using their mobile phones or sending e-mails on their laptops. This lacks professional etiquette, but at the same time if they feel they are wasting their time, invariably they will turn to other tasks which they deem to be more of a priority.

Lastly, the last agenda item: AOB (Any Other Business). I have seen this 'shopping list' and often added by colleagues who missed the agenda items deadline! The AOB item may have an operational focus, rather than anything strategic, but it should be a pertinent matter relevant to the immediate or coming week rather than agreeing a deadline or date for staff training, for example, which should be agreed well in advance.

Accountability

Many (expensive) courses on leadership development emphasise 'holding others to account' and 'having difficult conversations'. They focus on your authority in your role. They stress how you hold others to task to ensure objectives are met, lagging performance challenged and in worse case scenarios, having to 'move staff on'. These are very necessary conversations and needed in a leader's toolkit for sure.

Furthermore, these courses leave you with emotive 'one liners' such as: "children only get one chance" or "underperformance must be challenged" or "you cannot defend the indefensible" (usually when referring to poor teaching, but they tend to overlook the shoddy recruitment, staff development and inadequate training that led to the poor teaching). However, there is a risk, as a leader, you can lose sight of your own position. 'Telling' others is easy but telling yourself is not so. As leaders we should ensure self-accountability. Consider this from another perspective. How many headteachers reflect and realise the role is too much for them and 'step down' to SLT or even return to teaching?

Instead, how is it that many 'failed' Headteachers, Principals and senior school leaders seem to go on to be in leadership in other schools with a trail of inadequacy covered in bluff? It is a strong term "failed". By this I mean having been in a school in a position of leadership for at least 3 to 4 years with no consistent evidence of improvement of increased student achievement, enhanced teacher performance, or an increase in positive behaviour for learning, to name but three domains. How often are they recycled? In the past, this was by the LEA (Local Education Authority) appointed as a Headteacher elsewhere. If unable to get a foothold to cause damage in another school, they became a SIP (School Improvement Partner) advising schools on behalf of the LEA.

These days, more usually, failing Heads or Principals are redistributed within the MAT (Multi-Academy Trust) to lead or advise other school leaders despite a CV of near inept, incompetent school leadership which is marketed and branded as a "strong track record in leadership" on the corporate website. Or they relocate (overseas) and assume a Headship with little due diligence of their prior track record or even worse, they reinvent themselves to lead workshops on effective leadership!

Only one Education Secretary in England had the dignity to step down from the role[4] when she felt unable to fulfil this great responsibility. Note, she is the one of a very small minority who had been a qualified teacher and had attended a state (Government funded) school.

B

Blind ambition

Blind ambition, also known as backstabbing or betrayal can appear and disappear throughout your career when circumstances change or opportunities present themselves, especially in testing times or moments of desperation.

You have become a leader for a reason usually a combination of ambition, ability, aptitude and possibly academic (or professional) qualifications underpinned with effort and hard work. Leaders are very driven. However, taking this literally: learning to drive and being a good driver are two different matters.

Reflect on your journey to leadership and all of your promotions to date. If you have a clear conscience and no regret - Brilliant! Keep leading with the moral purpose[5] that you have espoused. If there is any nagging doubt that some element of deceit or duplicity has taken place, be sure to temper your ambition with some level of humility going forward.

Ambition ought to lead to success. Indeed, to be successful, assume more responsibility and thus have an impact over a broader scope of the school community which is something worthy of celebration; a vindication of ambition it could be argued. Unlike the corporate world, where it tends to be linked to financial reward, education is meant to be about improving the life chances of children.

With this fundamental belief, in conjunction with the team of adults in the school organisation and effective strategic partnerships, there is a genuine hope that your ambition for success for all students will indeed fulfil the aspiration of the parents and carers of the children who entrust you with their children.

The career development also more crudely known as promotion in school leadership does lead to headship for many (though the staff workforce census in England, and also as seen in the senior leadership teams of many international schools shows clear underrepresentation in some demographics such as ethnicity). Yet that blind ambition can result in types of Headteachers/Principals whose impact in levelling the playing field for all children is one of a missed opportunity.

Many school leaders keep moving around to climb to the 'top' and then some stereotypes of headteachers emerge. Indeed, the Harvard Business Review (HBR) identified Five Headteacher types (Surgeon, Philosopher, Architect, Accountant, Soldier) in research published in October 2016[6] (albeit in 'turnaround' schools and with a sample of just over 400 out of more than 20,000 headteachers in England).

However, I will group the school leaders into my own five categories based upon observations and interactions over the past two decades:

Principled: Principals with principles are sadly in a small minority at present. They do make a difference for others (rather than a difference to their bank balance as they often are paid less than their peers). Often sailing against the political tide, they are committed to the school's long-term improvement and support the profession itself. They develop staff to have the same commitment as themselves for the students and in doing so, grow staff in their career pathways. Such leaders tend to work in deprived communities if working in Britain or work in not-for-profit schools internationally.

Puppets: The ones who are 'puppet Principals' who work in a 'franchised school' by which I mean a MAT (Multi-Academy Trust in England) or a group of schools belonging to one corporate group in the international scene who answer the call to their Executive Headteacher or Director of Education rather than have their own leadership style: the 80:20 rule, 80% dictated and 20% autonomy. Budget allocation and staff structures 'centrally managed' under the guise of efficiency, but, for control, resulting in these Headteachers being a senior manager rather than a senior leader.

Politician: The ones who regularly attend conferences, or are keynote speakers, fully focussed on being 'out of school' and the centre of attention constantly developing their public image. They will gladly delegate everything to their Deputy or Vice-Principal and assume a politician role in the media – eager to give their opinion and sit on committees, but less eager to be in school, running a school.

Mercenaries: The ones who are 'careers Heads' and move from school to school every 2-3 years before their results 'catch up with them'. In their first year of tenure, they will take credit for any inherited success as having had 'immediate impact' or on the contrary blame the predecessor to justify their intended changes. Then in the second year in post, they begin to bring about significant change publicised as 'developing the green shoots of success'. In the third year, they focus on their own job applications and thus detract from their actual role as a school leader by spending so much (working) time and emotional effort in completing applications and attending interviews. They may justify their eventual departure by saying they have 'improved' the school, but the legacy tends to be a downward slide of poor succession planning (as it was always about themselves only) akin to the Surgeon or the Accountant from the HBR research.

Retired: The ones waiting to retire and tend to be leading 'coasting' schools. They delegate to anyone else (usually to take a tax-free second pension overseas in the for-profit education scene after decades of working in the publicly funded schools in the UK or USA).

Whilst we are all flawed humans and indeed ambition is very much a personal as much as a professional need in many cases, ambition should not be composed of 'playing' the role. Being upright with some moral purpose, is of course, better done if it is genuine. Talking a good talk or being caught out as you clasp the ladder of promotion will not only leave debris and casualties along the way, but it tarnishes a well-earned reputation. In worse case scenarios, some of these 'giants' of school leadership end up wrapped up in their ego and charges of nepotism and even financial irregularity appear as a shadow as they take early retirement (usually by starting a consultancy group).

It is far better to be collaborative and cooperative as this has longer term payoff than short-term gains by being conniving or cunning!

Building
The 'Academic' and 'non-Academic' is the classic denial of responsibility a school leader makes in an almost secular stance that "this is not my domain" and quickly scuttles back to their office or calls the cleaner, caretaker/site manager to "deal with it".

As a school leader, care for the building, the school site, as you would care for your own car or home. It is the home for hundreds of children and young people for a third of their day for 5 days a week in a term which amounts to nearly a quarter of their calendar year in school or a quarter of their childhood and adolescent life!

As a teacher of mathematics, I had to ensure this book has a calculation and here it is:
- Assume a third of a day is in school which would incorporate travel time to and from school x 5 days in a school week x 37 weeks in a school year = 61.7 days.
- Assuming a third of the day is set aside for sleep, this leaves 243 days in the 'awake' year.
- 61.7 ÷ 243 x 100 = 25.3% of the days awake in the year is spent in school.

The middle leader (e.g. Head of Subject or Head of Year/House) is rightly very territorial about their team and classrooms, corridors, labs and/or learning spaces. The senior leader must extrapolate this ethos to the school as an entirety.

This does not mean walking around with a radio akin to a security guard, (I have been there and it is not the best way!), but rather having that sense of purpose to help ensure the site is safe, purposeful and a great climate for learning.

As a senior school leader, you teach a lot less and have more 'non-contact' time as we say in this profession. Use the time to walk around the site on daily basis and not only when it is your 'duty day'. There is something that can be said about MBWA (management by walking around), which can be traced back to some American companies in the 1970s![7] It provides a raw and informal view of the school, much like unannounced learning walks to quality assure what is happening in the classroom. Your visit around the site also provides a 'fresh eyes' approach to site issues. It also builds up your presence in the school, especially if you are new, to ensure you gain that broader understanding of the school site and 'to be seen' by all colleagues rather than by only those in your immediate sphere of influence. You are a school leader rather than a line manager of a few select staff.

The first 100 days in your role is where you will see the most things. Make a note each day before you finish onsite and head home. After which, the dented cupboard, the door with the broken handle soon fades into your subconscious and the background.

You owe it to the students first and foremost and to colleagues that you keep a vigilant eye for health and safety. However, also for opportunities for innovation and refurbishment (hopefully more than the annual summer wall painting top up)! This can also be further reinvigorated with research from other schools and learning environment updates. (Refer to Chapter Q.)

Budget

Now you are a school leader you will have more say in what is being spent and where and when. The ability to approve or sign off on 'requests' for CPD (Continuous Professional Development), ICT (Information and Communication Technology, more commonly known as 'technology') or any other resources is a great privilege. If you are new to Headship, then the chances are, you will be setting the budget as well as allocating the budget to your SLT and line managers.

A common 'mistake' or misjudgement, especially new budget holders make, is to have 'early investment' i.e. a lot of front loading and high expenditure for the start of term 1. I have seen this resulting in exercise books running out by the end of term 3!

When faced with a large investment such as a new IT learning platform, a new curriculum with supporting resources or a new data analysis software, I would advise the following, from my experience of having gone down both routes: if you have to prioritise which to invest in (unless you have the rare luxury of an unlimited budget!): staff or systems? I would lean towards staff. Training staff on how to use part of a platform well is better than trying to implement the whole platform with scant training.

Consider what the needs are for professional development versus the need for new systems. As school leaders, it is easy to accept verbal recommendations from peers within the school or in other 'leading' schools of what to use or implement. This risks a lack of due diligence for the context of the school you work in.

For example, a new data analysis system is to be implemented. This project may involve a 'core team' involving the IT manager, Exams/Data manager and maybe a Teacher Coach or Lead Teacher and coordinated by an Assistant Head. They all attend the specialist training with a plan to roll it out across the school in a day long staff INSET (In-Service Training). (These were introduced by the Education Minister Kenneth Baker in 1988 and were informally known as 'Baker Days'. They increased the Teachers' working year from 190 days to 195 with five mandatory INSET days.)

Yet the risks of the new data analysis system 'fading over time' is real. This is often because it is only understood by a few (in the core team) who have great technical knowledge and/or are tech or data enthusiasts. Should one of the core team leave, gaps in the use of this new system or platform soon appear, with inefficient, ineffective and incomplete use of the platform, until it is replaced yet again with the same delivery roll out risks. Instead, consider the purpose and timing of the training for all staff. Do they all need to be trained at the same time? Is there a school specific training manual or a generic help guide form the supplier? Are there advocates in each curriculum team to ensure the platform is fully embedded?

A system is only as good as the people expected to uphold it. By investing in quality, competent staff with excellent professional development opportunities, it provides the means to further ensure quality teaching and learning: the 'core business' or the main purpose of a school!

Thankfully, schools have moved away from costly CPD from the 'expert' (by a former school leader who became a self-appointed 'expert' but often several years retired and really out of touch with current practice or the 'one size fits all' day of CPD where all staff are sat in the hall and the bigger concern is what is for lunch rather than what is being presented on the 'screen'.

Also, with more challenging budgets, school leaders have had to be more innovative with what they have available to spend on professional learning and development. This has resulted in a lot more 'in-house' CPD with more school-specific relevance rather than a generic tool trying to provide a bespoke solution. This has produced a culture of 'champions' from within the school, a home-grown band of enthusiasts, if not experts, who can further the cause of a particular initiative.

This is a useful approach and worth considering for you, as a school leader, in an allocated remit such as leading on professional development. Seek out the competent, enthusiastic colleagues who will be able to grow and thrive and support your strategy or plan.

C

Change

Change occurs in schools more often than many school leaders would prefer. Sometimes it is down to policy or framework changes, given to schools to implement. Other times it is down to the circumstances of the school i.e. staffing or building amendments. How you manage the change will determine how effective the change is and what damage or debris is left along the way if the change management was ineffective.

Templates and models exist to be used to support school development as do 'off the shelf' technology products. (Refer to Chapter T.) However, the challenge for a leader in any sector but especially in schools when leading change management, is to demonstrate transformational leadership. As a new leader, evaluate the context. The eagerness to demonstrate impact is to 'change the change' and prove to others (as well as yourself) that you are doing it 'your way'. (No Frank Sinatra pun intended!) However, change management is a training course. The bigger picture is always worth considering in the order of these paired questions:

Firstly	Secondly	Thirdly
Why?	What?	When?
Who?	How?	Where?

- *Why?* Why do you need to change? Is a slight modification or upgrade needed or does it have to be a system/policy overhaul?
- *Who?* Put this question out to your fiercest critics or least likely to change as Simon Sinek rightly identifies as the 'laggards' on the adoption curve from what he calls 'The Law of Diffusion of Innovation'.[8]

A vivid example I recall is when Interactive Whiteboards (IWB) became the new EdTech hardware that schools were implementing in the mid-2000s. Many staff used it as an 'EWB' rather than an IWB: an electronic whiteboard. They merely used it to write on with their stylus rather than its intended purpose: to make teaching and learning interactive. In most cases, this limited use of the IWB technology was not because of the 'technophobic dinosaurs' in schools, but rather the lack of training to explain the 'why?' IWB offer better methods for teaching than the conventional whiteboard or blackboard (depending which era you went to school). The 'experts' in the school and the trainers sent by the external manufacturers focus on the "how". How can you add a picture and annotate it? Rather than why add a picture and annotate? Or how can you make learning more interactive? When they ought to be asking teachers why make it more interactive?

Therefore, if these 'dinosaurs' have a 'winning formula' which at the turn of the century was based on three Es, Example, Explain, Exercises (hence the name exercise book); and have great student (exam) outcomes, why would they want to change their approach to teaching? What needs to change? In this example, the approach to teaching is outmoded in an interactive digital era for learners.

How can the training become personalised and relevant for different levels of teacher proficiency? In this example of IWB, the teacher who has gadgets and is a decade plus younger than colleagues in the department is almost expected to be the 'techy' one in the department. (I was one of those, tech enthusiasts who was the first teacher in my school to have a Personal Digital Assistant (PDA) Pocket PC in the mid-2000s and one of the first SLT to buy a tablet within a fortnight of its launch in the UK in 2010.)

Lastly, when and where are essential to ensure successful change. Timing is crucial. I have often used a two-term implementation from Spring to Summer (having previously evaluated in Autumn). School leaders make the mistake of the 'big launch' in August/September and staff are literally in the post-summer holiday mindset and not at their optimum to take in the big announcement. Consider the following timeline:

- Have a working group to discuss the proposed change in the second half of Term 1.
- Launch a pilot at the start of Term 2.

- Evaluate it in Term 3 and then consider if it needs full rollout or not.

The example of the IWB is a technology implementation and such a project can follow this timeline. However, if it is for example, a new reporting cycle, it can easily be trialled in one year group rather than a whole key stage or in one subject rather than all subjects etc. before full rollout.

Context

New leaders especially those who join new schools, make the faux pas of saying terms such as "in my previous school" and go on to say, "I did this and it was rated outstanding". To make matters worse, some (lazy) leaders forget to change the logo of the resource they are using or the date from their previous "outstanding" school setting!

Not only is it disrespectful to the community you are now leading, but asides from the patronising "I am the expert" or "I know better" it is an example of not understanding the context. What could indeed have been a successful model in your prior role needs adapting in your new context to enhance or build on any existing success. The best school leaders understand the context they are operating in. That is not to say that context cannot be changed over time, but rather if the past is understood, it is easier to challenge the present (status quo) and thus shape the future.

Context can be in so many ways, but more than likely it is interwoven with culture. Is context a result of culture or does context shape the culture? The obvious internal one is the performance of the school. What is going well must be celebrated and shared. What is not going well must be addressed and with a sense of urgency and seriousness that it deserves – a kind of PIPRIP (Praise in Public, Reprimand in Private). Yet other contexts can be more subtle such as the legacy of a particular department or faculty and the nuances in a particular cohort whether this is staff or students.

As school leaders, your decisions may be challenged openly though you may receive thanks from individual staff in private . . . CHIP-PIP Challenged in Public, Praised in Private. It is healthy to have such dialogue with staff, especially detractors, so long as it is out of professional respect and not from personal insulting.

Of course, you cannot expect to be a mind reader, but as a school leader it is essential to gain an understanding of the context of your school. This will help you to anticipate any barriers as you hope to deliver sustained improvement. It is too easy and dangerous to impose your world view on the community you are serving.

Mutual benefit and understanding with moral purpose are essential and will always stand you in good stead.[9] This myopic and cultural illiteracy leads to a lack of cultural capital and produces fallacies with sinister undertones of social engineering. For example, a child from a low-income household (previously known as 'working-class') ought to play a violin as a measure of refinement i.e. assuming 'middle class values'.

Consequently, you may see such great end results with media headlines such as "from the council estate to Cambridge". (Or any other 'elite' selective university, such as Oxford, Harvard, Yale etc. are also cited too.) What it does not show you is the impact on that child, now a teenager, that graduates as a young adult. It does not show you how the student may have 'forgotten their roots,' their family or community, in this pathway of socio-economic betterment and cultural assimilation.

What should have been a role model of success for their community, only reaffirms the notion that to be successful you need to adopt a new culture and not adapt in your context. Thus, this graduate can no longer relate to their community and seldom visits let alone interacts as they have friends in 'high places' now. This is a great example of how schools can act as social engineers rather than develop a social enterprise where a strong alumni and mentoring would create a culture of 'giving (back)'. Great school leaders instil this notion of community and service to all their students.

Collaborate

One of the most overused words in education, along with other words such as 'support', 'intervention' and 'progress'. However, if meant in the fullest sense, the operative word should be 'consult' with collective decision-making and in doing so provide an opportunity for other individuals and stakeholders to be involved in the direction of the school or organisation. Beyond the school gate, it is the intent to have a sector-wide vision and as a school leader, provide a worthy contribution to the dialogue on the future direction of policy and provision.

From the outside, an observation of the 'hierarchy' can provide an indication of the understanding of how the school functions. From the inside, the soon observed behavioural norms can identify how well staff work collaboratively. It also feeds into the classroom on how students learn. Is it a didactic approach? Or are students encouraged to deduce and reason, discuss and articulate their responses?

On a micro-level, staff practice can be perceived from lesson planning, resource preparation. A quick scan on the shared network drive can indicate this i.e. who has edit rights?! On an operational level, when cover is needed, how is it supported by others in the team? Scale this into inter-departmental practice and you can then deduce which subjects and faculties work together. Is it always the middle leader/team leaders or can teachers and staff in the departments also contribute or work together on a project etc?

In Senior Leadership, is it very much a vertical line management? "I lead this, I need to be cc'd in this e-mail" etc. or does the SLT help and support each other. The ineffective SLT, usually underscored by ongoing politics, becomes very territorial (with other underlying insecurities). When the 'greater good' or the 'bigger picture' should dictate the 'working together' practice in the school.

The more effective school leaders facilitate this by default and it results in autonomy and trust. Consequently, a sense of (healthy) risk-taking occurs. Similarly, by removing formal barriers, it allows a sense of freedom to operate across the school without the formal invitation. The contrary is true for the less effective leaders who adopt an almost command and control approach which hinders risk-taking and team members await to be told what to do.

As a new school leader, evaluate when the collaborative ethos can be fully implemented. Is it a case of removing all formalities and make it a free for all! Sometimes, a formal directive approach is needed to establish norms and expectations. However, the intent should be there to ensure this a stop in the journey whose destination should always be collaborative.

Collaboration will result in a shared success. Yet some selfish team leaders misuse this by some taking credit for other people's contributions. The 'show pony' may wear the rosette, but the team mucking up at the stable cannot be forgotten in helping produce this success. Schools are about people: Working together for one another. Any insecurity or fear of failure should be put aside. The more effective school leaders learn from mistakes and have the confidence to dare, try, reflect and improve, without the fear of failure. Effective school leaders share the success, or rather step aside to let others take centre stage in moments of success.

D

Deadlines

Accountability is not only ensuring staff perform, but also ensuring compliance with due dates. The heroic 'stay up all night' to complete the school reports, to plan lessons, or to finish the inspection preparation may achieve short-term objectives, but it indicates a lack of adequate planning and preparation especially around time management. There should not be any last minute or 'overdue deadlines' that result in such excessive work into the night.

Deadlines that are set for the start of the working week provide an implicit expectation of working over the weekend. Similarly, having a deadline at the end of the week and then moving it over the weekend implies the first deadline was not sufficient.

From a leadership aspect, there is an implicit and explicit deadline. The former is when you expect something to be completed and this is the date you should refer to publicly. It does allow for leeway for any unforeseen or unexpected circumstances such as staff absence, system malfunction or a school closure.

Weather closures vary around the world. In the UK, this could be a 'snow day' but in could be a 'rain day' in schools in the Gulf! Explicit deadlines for known events are due: i.e. payment for an order, or reports to be sent to parents, or when the inspectors are due to visit the school (albeit with increasingly shorter notice periods).

In either circumstance, implicit or explicit deadlines, plan well ahead. Many school leaders make the mistake of what I call 'cyclical weekly deadlines'. This has the very real risk of what I call the 'domino deadline delay' effect. If the first deadline is not met, the chances are the second and subsequent deadlines will not be met. A knock-on effect.

For example, consider the approach to the (old) school reporting cycle and add the layer of risk management:

Week 5 Assess students: Insufficient time to assess (mark) the students' work. Consider which subjects/types of assessments need to be scheduled where in the assessment timetable.

Week 6 Input data and verify datasheets: The delay from the previous week will mean a delay in the inputting of the data. Also training needs could have been identified to avoid "I thought I had saved the data" response from specific staff who are overdue with their data. This puts more pressure on department leads to verify and validate the data input.

Week 7 Draft reports: The knock-on effect of incomplete or missing data. Reports cannot be drafted with the due time needed.

Week 8 Proof reports and publish: If less time is available to proof, the risk of error and rushing for publication is immense. This can lead to disastrous public displays of inadequacy such as having to reissue reports with accurate data or statements on it.

This (old) system risks providing three-week old historic data published possibly four weeks later. Thankfully, many schools these days, have 'real time' reporting solutions with online reporting tools. However, I say 'old' in parentheses as it is still sadly current in many schools too. Deadlines therefore need to be managed in context and not just as a calendar exercise.

Common deadlines in schools are lesson observations/teacher evaluations and assessments/student evaluations. Both can be improved by having more efficient systems to remove or reduce the administration blockage that such systems demand in recording, inputting, or typing up content.

Other deadlines such as expected action points from meetings must be such that team members can accomplish these in time. However, to enable this to happen from your perspective, you should consider a communicated deadline and an actual deadline. For example, ensure the feedback or action which is needed is given two working days before you 'actually' need it. Send a two working day reminder before this also, so in effect the recipient has a four working day lag and so do you if it overruns i.e. due on Friday, but set the deadline for Wednesday and send a reminder on Monday.

The personal approach is worth the time and effort to visit the person and remind them and then follow up on e-mail, on the record, so any reminder is not lost in the busy nature that schools are. The reminders tend to be via e-mail or alerts. Yet I would suggest having a personalised message rather than a standard alert notification.

Data literate

Data: too much, too often and too little used and usually misinterpreted! As systems used in schools become almost wholly digital, we gather more and more data, it can literally become data for the sake of data. In the (old) days, what used to be a class register, a mark book and the annual handwritten report with one or two formal lesson observations (also handwritten in real time) has now become a plethora of online systems to not only maintain, but to refer to daily.

Assessment data needs to be timely and not merely for exam hothousing. The mistake new school leaders risk making is to focus on the 'borderline' students. Of course, schools in challenging circumstances know too well that marginal gains in areas of focus could be the difference between 'passing' or 'failing' an inspection. (Such is the awful terminology of perception of schools.)

Data literacy is the ability to understand, analyse and present or communicate data in a coherent and relevant way for the audience. School leaders will delegate such tasks to the data manager to produce colourful charts with little involvement other than presenting. (It can result in embarrassing episodes such as politicians who get percentages in a muddle due to a passive involvement in the data!)

Nor should we have a culture of 'checking the checking' but all effective school leaders should be comfortable in calculating an average, a % change or adding a formula in a spreadsheet and providing their own interpretation as a school leader depending on the audience:

- 'Headline figures' (akin to an Executive Summary) for the Board of Governors
- By department for the SLT
- By the group of teachers for the MLT
- By class/cohort for the teacher

Most of this will be presented and summarised by the data system in the school and prepared by the data manager or by applying a filter on a system.

However, data literacy is more than presenting data analysis. It should be about identifying trends, patterns, outliers and why this is the case and what can be done to achieve or exceed targets. This is where the data literate school leader adds great value to a school with their insight and suggested actions as a result of what the data shows.

For example, comparing this year to previous years; or dig deeper to compare gender, EAL, SEND, ethnicity year on year; between subjects and even from starting points in primary to end points in secondary to have a true picture of longitudinal progress over time (over 11 or 13 years of school).

It helps form a picture of learning outcomes, but also an evaluation of curriculum leadership and teacher performance. It should inform training needs and which staff 'perform the best' for which cohort. The great school leaders look at longitudinal data as well as research beyond the school to pick up trends.

Furthermore, data science is becoming increasingly important. The more we know, the more we can provide solutions or, so we are told. How can school leaders provide data-backed evidence for a proposed change?

Looking at the skills of the future,[10] what is being done to modify the curriculum to enable future learners to develop skills such as 'joining the dots'.

Delegation

By being more senior, you have authority over more people; both directly and indirectly. The key is to delegate for task completion, but also to acknowledge others. The better school leaders go on to develop others also. A great school leader can see the strengths and areas of development for the wider team.

Whereas the unscrupulous school leader delegates the task and when complete is first to announce it to the staff as their own achievement: "I have done this data analysis" (when clearly the file shows it was last modified by . . . the Data admin!) Or for the sake of self-preservation blame someone else if failings arise and even worse remove them from the team or organisation as a scapegoat. This is both unethical and immoral.

Inevitably, new school leaders turn to those they know (or trust) for task delegation and completion. This can risk being seen as a clique and closed-door approach that the same individuals are chosen. Whilst it is for convenience, efficiency or reliability reasons which are all a valid rationale; as you grow in your role, the challenge is to develop others.

Similarly, taking the blame for the mistake or blunders of others (especially in teams you lead or manage) is noble but bruising. Yet allowing others to fall and helping them back up is more developmental in the long run. Patience and accepting there will be setbacks and mistakes should be considered when developing others. You and your colleagues whom you line manage, mentor or coach also need to learn to stand up after crawling before walking let alone running!

Another issue facing new school leaders is 'letting go' of previous responsibilities. This is very real especially in internal promotion to SLT within your current school setting. In a new school setting, it is a risk that you 'tread on toes' as you may have a preference in your previous role in care and guidance, but your new role is more focused on assessment, but it is too easy to become too involved in the domain of the previous role even though there is someone else responsible for it.

It is difficult as you progress in leadership to learn to trust others to take the full ownership. Yet it is needed. Successors may do things differently to you but that is their right to do so.

E

Equity

Not as in shares of a company, (but I do wonder if this could work in the profit-making international schools' scene, to become a profit-sharing entity in the form of a teachers' cooperative?) but rather a school leader must ensure equity for every person. This makes the great leaders stand out from the 'trained managers' (who seldom change their mindset or adapt their practice despite the leadership learning received on the leadership courses they attended but are quick to boast about their new leadership qualifications).

Equality is sometimes mistaken for equity. Equity is ensuring the opportunities are afforded for all students to achieve; or for all staff to develop. It does mean making difficult decisions on the priorities. Some will need greater assistance than others. Some will need elevating whilst others are not necessarily held back but rather expected to make their progress on their own (for a particular period of time).

Know every person, give them your time. More so if you are new to a school, make the first 100 days count by immersing yourself in the school community. If you are in your role because of an internal promotion, also make the first 100 days count by establishing conversation and dialogue with staff whom you have never or rarely spoken with; it may be the support staff who you may smile at occasionally, in the corridor as you quickly move on by.

Leadership must be embedded and not with a superficial presence or "this is what I did in my previous school" rhetoric and you merely impose this template on the school. Great school leaders provide opportunities for all. They can train the trainer and in doing so deploy key staff to help upskill the whole school community. It is about having the intent to gain a thorough insight of the school community and going about it to make it happen.

A good way to achieve this is to provide an audience for all the staff. This is something I did in two schools I led. Arrange to meet each staff (teaching and non-teaching) for 15 minutes in the first term of your role. Listen to them and ask them to tell you about themselves, share their story. Then if it has not been covered during their story, ask three pertinent questions: What is going well? What two things could be improved? Where do you see yourself in 3 years' time?

This provides a personal interaction and provides an invaluable insight into your community, their needs, hopes, fears and ambition. It essentially enables an audit of the staff community too. It is a major commitment in the first term of your headship or senior leadership, but it pays dividends further on in the long term in your people management.

Further down the road in your tenure, ensure you provide a follow-up opportunity with all staff too in a year or two's time. It shows sincerity in listening, hopefully acting upon and then reviewing with the staff who suggested the idea in the first place.

E-mail

How many e-mails a day? Do you ever switch off from e-mails? Or do you have them on your mobile phone and work through them in the evening, at the weekend and even on holiday (even abroad)? I would certainly advise against having e-mails on your phone. It naturally extends the (virtual) work environment into the (physical) home domain. This often means the phone/work comes first in place of your family, who do have a right to have you and your presence at home. This also sets expectations for your team members who will be senior line managers and for the wider workforce too.

'Zero inbox' may not be a reality. (An e-mail inbox folder with no e-mails by the end of each day. Replied to, deleted, forwarded to others, or perhaps archived.) However, e-mails are a good indication of the culture in the school. Is it healthy or toxic? If they are being sent late into the night and even replied to in the early hours, what does this say?

I recall having an e-mail dialogue regarding a disagreement with another member of SLT around 1am to 2am in the working week. It did not resolve anything, but rather I went to work the next day ready to continue the discussion with an emotional tinge which blurred my judgement at that time, wanting to prove a point etc.

Have and enforce an 'out of hours' policy on e-mail etiquette which will protect all staff and set out expectations that it is not acceptable to be e-mailing at night. Train staff to schedule e-mails to be sent in the hours of the working day. Ironically, it may mean a dozen e-mails arrive in your inbox in perfect sync at 8am!

If you are being cc'd (carbon copy); is it for a political reason or a practical reason? As a senior line manager (or 'the senior line manager' if a Headteacher or Principal) in your organisation, you should consider discussing in person (not via e-mail, as that would be ironic!) with the sender as to why you need to be cc'd.

Sometimes it is for the sender to stress the importance of being witness to or informed of something. Other times it is the threat that the person has cc'd the senior leader/head to make a point. An example is a reminder e-mail "this is just a polite reminder; data is due on . . ". There is nothing polite of having to cc their line manager or a senior leader in an e-mail to a staff member. Of course, cc e-mails may be needed for the record, for accountability etc.

Yet it is a judgement call of how many to be cc'd on, by who and when and for what purpose. Given e-mails are formal communication on the record, copies of the e-mails can always be forwarded afterwards. For example, if it is about having an audit trail for a performance management discussion with someone rather than be cc'd in the first instance.

Meanwhile, if you feel the need or are having to be bcc'd (blind carbon copy) then this is a very toxic culture and sets a dangerous precedent on the lack of trust and transparency. This is one for a new school leader to avoid and one where behaviours and norms of an organisation can be challenged and changed from the outset of your tenure. If others like to bcc, you do not need to stoop so low.

The other aspect of e-mails is that you are in a position of great authority. E-mail etiquette extends to how you respond or send e-mails in the first instance. As school leaders you do not always need to have the final say (I have been there and it comes down to petty points scoring and saps energy and diverts you from the focus and matter at hand).

Having a right to reply or having the last say (or more often than not, the first and last say) to initiate or terminate a dialogue is not always needed. Is the e-mail to provide information, an update or to challenge? Sometimes a brief response of confirming acknowledgement can provide tremendous reassurance to the sender.

The more senior you become, the less is said on e-mail to avoid recrimination further down the road. Communicating in person, human face to face communication (as opposed to video conferencing) has more merit. Also, whatever is said on e-mail should be with the intent of being honest and purposeful and not dishonest and superficial.

Envy

It is not a race of who of your peers becomes a Headteacher or a Principal before you! As you progress in your career, you will meet many others whom you may have worked with or attended the same leadership training and whose 'online status' updates shows they have gone on to assume a Headship or become an advisor for the Government in less than a decade. Too often this is a result of the ego, or the person feels insecure for being in a position 'behind' or 'below' their peers and not quite fulfilling their own ambition (to date).

As a new school leader, look away from others and look at your own path. How did you get here and by which method and approach did you achieve this? As mentioned in Chapter B, the persona (or 'mask worn' to use an acting reference) of the headteacher and the overambitious school leader may get them far and high up the ladder, but you need to focus on your own development and career aspirations and ambition rather than feel envy or jealous about other contemporaries.

Grace and dignity will always come out on top especially when you are facing those challenges and uncertainty of what role to do next and when to achieve it. This is very much a 'what lies beneath' reflection. (Edward Hall's book emphasised that values and thought patterns are often hidden but clearly affect behaviours.) You became a teacher to help children, you became a school leader to help adults to help children. The helping and giving takes precedence over the taking and not helping.

The unscrupulous leaders boasting about exaggerated or false claims, promotions and achievements, can rattle anyone with insecurities, more so in this era of online social media with the FOMO (fear of missing out). Once insecure, you become vulnerable and even desperate. Subsequently your actions, comments and thoughts could easily become quite irrational. Push away from envy. It is healthy to be competitive, to have goals, drive and ambition.

Fulfilling the ambition for others (students and staff) is a way to achieve your ambition. Indeed those 'junior' to you may go on to assume roles that you had wished for, or even as I say many teacher and school leaders have not studied at 'leading universities' but they ought to be really pleased if students in their schools go on to study at some of the best universities in the world or join professions which bestow great rewards and benefits.

F

Feedback

Providing feedback on a lesson observation or on an initiative becomes more critical in your role. The 'not knowing' can lead to a very disenfranchised colleague. Or worse the disingenuous or ambiguous feedback "the lesson was fine" (when the overall lesson was not good) or "that was very good" (when the event was at best acceptable) without being more transparent or honest. This can also damage your reputation in both the short and medium term too within the organisation. Part of the challenge on feedback (to a lesson observation) is that you may find yourself having to provide feedback from a meeting or a joint lesson observation.

The first advice is to avoid feedback on feedback! Agree on the overall judgement with your co-observer i.e. strengths and successes as well as any areas of development, even if you both had different 'lenses' through which you were observing the lesson.

My second advice is not to offer indirect feedback via the subject leader, or sometimes the other way around, relay feedback from the subject leader back to the colleague in a messenger capacity. This cheapens the process and allows the unscrupulous school leader to manipulate feedback for their own agenda. If the effort was made for a joint lesson observation, then the effort should be made for a joint feedback session in person (or via video conference at least in these digital times!) and follow up with an e-mail so it is on the record rather than what was said behind closed doors.

The timing of the feedback is important. It should be timely and certainly in the same working week. Any delay will similarly lose the respect of the staff member if you literally observe and 'forget' to feedback as you were 'too busy'.

Feedback should be a transactional process, a two-way street. In an almost 'always on(line)' culture, it is a challenge to find that space to show considered feedback. However, the time and space must be provided to enable the response after the hours of preparation the staff made for a 40/50-minute lesson observation. Consider Inspector training, as it offers not only evaluative skills, but also the method to give succinct and effective feedback (usually by the end of the day).

Response rates can be perceived from the role of the person asking for feedback. If you are expected to feedback or provide an update to your line manager i.e. Principal (if you are SLT) or Governing Board (if you are the Principal), is your response more rapid or prioritised in a bid to impress because the person giving the feedback is more 'important' than you? Yet when the feedback or request for some information is from someone more 'junior' to you i.e. a teacher observed, do you then delay the response?

Joint feedback also provides genuine developmental feedback for the staff observed as well as a professional obligation to ask the staff member how they felt about the lesson. It allows you as the senior line manager to also gauge the effectiveness of the middle leader/subject leader in being able to have difficult conversations but also on how they provide developmental feedback too.

If the staff member being observed disagrees with your observations and judgement, what do you do? Do you react or respond to the comments which goes against your lesson judgement? Is it because of your own ignorance of not knowing (perhaps due to the subject not being in your specialist curriculum area) or do you simply overrule them due to your authority? Controlling any emotional or initial reaction is essential. Sometimes the non-verbal response is what is remembered most in the feedback environment.

Be gracious and have dignity especially in difficult conversations. The risk to use your authority to create enmity or worse to destroy a colleague based on the authority of your judgement can have serious ramifications for the future. Being two-faced and slamming the lesson in what you think is a private audience of peers but then giving a false narrative back to the staff member will sully and tarnish your reputation too. It does not need to be sugar-coated, but nor does it need to be blunt where people's self-esteem and their perception of you can be damaged.

How about when roles are reversed and you are receiving feedback? Consider the audience. This will demonstrate whether you are able to have an equitable approach to feedback. What is meant by this? If it is from your line manager, (i.e. Board of Governors if you are a Principal or if you are SLT from the Principal), do you accept the feedback even if it is with some criticism? Or if the audience is from an external body i.e. Inspectors, do you respond in an aggressively disagreeing manner if the feedback is different to what you expected?

Receiving feedback especially if it does not validate your position or point of view can cause a sense of tension and derail the narrative you intended to provide. However, it is worth making a note and rather than "I disagree with what you say", acknowledge as a valid perception from the staff member concerned. When they speak about how they felt the lesson fared, be active in listening, rather than waiting to give your feedback from your notes. There is nothing more offensive, when a staff member is feeding back, than a leader being so arrogant as to browse through their notes instead whilst the staff member is speaking.

It is worth considering having a 360-degree stakeholder survey in your first term and have the same survey with the same stakeholders in the third term of your tenure. This will allow you to evaluate your leadership and with the feedback from others to see how it matches your perception of your own leadership (development) over time.

Friends

If I had to describe effective leadership traits; they would be friendly and personable but not personal. It is too easy not to become a robotic leader focused on process and policy and at best make 'small talk' with colleagues i.e. discussing the football scores from the weekend on a Monday morning, but then ignore the colleague unless it is deadline-driven or work-related. Take an active interest in the person, value whatever they may share such as their family events; perhaps discussing teaching their child to learn how to ride a bike. It may appear trivial to you, but it matters to them and make that effort to be personable and have an interest.

Yet aside from being friendly, as a leader you need friends. Leadership can be very lonely at times. School leadership more so. The pressure and expectations are almost relentless as each academic year brings a new cohort of students to progress and pass through the school; trying to fulfil the dreams of hundreds of students, the aspirations of double the number of parents and enable the ambitions of all staff to be achieved all in a 40-week academic year.

Despite bearing this great burden on your shoulders, it is essential to have professional advice from mentors and I would advise you consider having leadership coaches if only to sound off to a neutral person outside of your organisation. Recently I received some great advice about not falling into "mind traps". Now with the benefit of hindsight, I should have had this advice much earlier in my leadership career. This would have prevented a lot of avoidable arguments, animosity and awkward conversations.

Even the informal friends outside of education, can also provide a perspective for you to air your thoughts and have some much-needed respite in your professional discourse. Many of the issues you face are to do with people management, interaction and communication with colleagues; what has been said, how it has been understood and what are the responses thereafter.

As you grow into school leadership, you will come across others and build that professional network. Having a trusted sounding board, always provides that sense of making the best considerations and more importantly, able to adapt your decision-making if the best intentions are not realised in the way intended.

By default, those friends within the profession will offer the best insight and have empathy and even had similar experiences. What is more telling is that as your career develops, especially in testing times, you can literally count your friends on your hand (or 'hands' if you are truly fortunate to have more than five genuine friends) who look out for you in times of significant challenge.

Whether you are going through a challenge, a major incident, or one with serious consequences (such as inspection downgrade) where your job is on the line or you have been moved on, or what is more common these days resigned before being moved on, (it is always a matter of perspective if you are pushed or jumped!), you can see who your real friends in the profession.

At best, most may say 'this is awful' and offer a 'good luck' or 'best wishes' message, but you could be in a very dark or lonely space. You could be feeling very vulnerable and the stages of grief could kick in; shock, anger, denial and before getting to acceptance. Your true friends would have spared some time for you . . . to listen to your concerns and grievances, first and foremost, but also to support, to advise, to counsel, to mentor and if you are fortunate to provide an opportunity for you to rebuild your career elsewhere.

Be sure to reciprocate this kindness when your true friends are in times of need. I acknowledged a few at the start of this book, but I could name dozens more, (but some of whom did not want to be named,) who have provided sound, confidential advice and support in my more private moments throughout my career.

Fitness

Health and wellbeing priorities must be kept as a daily reminder for you and your context, whether these are physical, psychological (i.e. mental, or emotional) or even spiritual (i.e. keeping your values refreshed and energised). These are essential for anyone to be effective.

There is a cost of leadership as much as there is a price of leadership. Many leaders may 'pay the price' and resign or be fired from their organisation, but that is merely a salaried job which they will begin again elsewhere. Seldom is the cost of leadership elaborated. Cost is certainly in terms of time, emotion and sacrifice. The time spent on the job, in lieu of time with family or friends.[11] The emotional commitment to the job with its great responsibility risks long-term damage on your effectiveness as a committed, dedicated school leader. Consequently, the very real risk of becoming cynical in the professional domain and neglectful in your personal life are very real: a diet misbalance, a lack of sleep, emotional tension in your family space can lead to risks of some form of long-term damage in your personal life.

Evaluate your daily routine. It can literally be a diary of your working week and even the weekend. If your working day begins with a caffeine shot and checking e-mails and your diary before the daily walk around, where is the space for you? Keeping fit and healthy is as much in your work habits as it is in your lifestyle in general.

How often on a leadership training course are some of your peers able to focus on the physical health aspect? They could be the eager swimmer, cyclist, runner, or gym attendee up before dawn and completed a full workout. Whilst this is impressive and it is not just down to those individuals expressing their competitive edge or desire to compete and win, (although this is the reason why alpha male/female dominance tends to be a bias in leadership representation,) it is important to have a physical health focus on yourself in a regular and sustained way. Not everyone can be the county or national champion triathlete but have a sporting or physical activity to ensure your body's health supports the wellbeing of your mind.

As a school leader, you risk being sedentary in an office; managing by e-mails and hosting meetings which reinforce an inactive work habit which in turn becomes a habit that extends beyond the school gates. E.g. risks extending into your lifestyle; return home and lie on the couch watching a streaming channel.

However, not only could the lack of brain oxygen inhibit clear thinking, but the health damage could be longer term and 'suddenly' appear having built up over decades. The analogy of the overflowing water in the sink is worthy to note. The water was building up over time, why allow it to spill, when you had opportunities to drain the water?

School leaders must take care of students, staff and increasingly support the families of the students. If you are unhealthy and unable to function effectively, the risk to the wider school community is amplified.

Look after yourself, so you can look after others.

G

Generosity

Are you a good leader or a great leader? A theme throughout this book. Most school leaders can train or learn to become a good leader or as I say a 'good manager' in a school or any organisation. Dedication, effort and honesty should help you achieve this. However, great leaders give in every sense of the word. The obvious two are time and money, but there are many more aspects where you can give as a leader.

Generosity should not be taught or learned. It is in human nature. Children are by their very nature kind and sharing. For example, the hungry boy, who was clearly living in severe poverty, in Sierra Leone in 2010, who was given two lollipops by the photographer but then instinctively gave one back to the photographer.[12] Yet as many children grow up, especially in more developed economies and consumer societies, are taught to be selfish and prejudiced by poor parenting, inadequate education and also inequity they face in society and the world around them.

Time in the workplace is the most obvious one as a leader. Whilst your schedule is very precious, making time, 'finding time' or sparing it for others will go a long way in terms of impact and expectation.

Charity in the form of donating money in your personal life, but also you giving by way of sharing your experiences, working knowledge and life skills to others, as a mentor to aspiring leaders or as a colleague to support the team. Buy a lunch and catch up with colleagues.

School finances should ensure staff wellbeing is seen as an investment and not a (sunk) cost. A (free) 'lunch and learn' professional learning activity is always well received by colleagues. Where school budgets are more miserly, it reflects as much on the school leadership and management as it does on the school itself. If you are in such a school, ensure frugality does not hinder the 'investment' in staff. What should be avoided is to promise many things at the start of term, but when it comes to delivery or actualisation, get them on the cheap so they do not last or worse have many unfulfilled promises or pledges.

The recent pandemic has only emphasised how great schools, led by great leaders, value staff and put staff wellbeing as a priority (as well as student wellbeing). The opposite is sadly true. The less generous (or neglectful) school leaders are more concerned about compliance or conforming to their authority and 'rule with fear'. The net result is staff morale is decimated and staff turnover is likely to be high. What is more telling is when such less generous (insincere) leaders give (and make a point of giving i.e. cakes for all staff), is it received as a cynical ploy by the staff?

The tragic thing about this is such superficial leaders are so out of touch with events on the ground that they do not know how poorly they are perceived by staff. Their ignorance and their arrogance of self-importance has blinded them in their miserliness. This is also a trait for a real-life example of the Dunning-Kruger effect as such individuals tend to be incompetent in other areas, but they do not know that they do not know! A cognitive bias where people overestimate their own ability or knowledge.[13]

Emotional generosity can be so easy to donate. Give a greeting and avoid falling into the trap of self-importance or only wanting to speak to someone when you need them to do something. The usual brisk walk past the corridor or as I call it the 'photocopied smile' (or grimace even,) as you walk past your colleague in the school corridor is very disingenuous. Acknowledgement and recognition go a long way. Nobody wants to be ignored! Of course, the formal end of term or colleague of the month is one way to recognise and give praise. However, a daily "how are you?" or at the start of a working week to ask, "how was your weekend?" This shows personal interest and care and can actually add great value to staff being valued.

Growth

Effective school leaders need to have a 'growth mindset'[14] to grow as a person and as a professional. School leaders risk reaching what they perceive to be 'optimum performance'. Successful strategies used in a previous school and applied again with a similar level of success provides the risk of preliminary conclusions that this methodology 'always works'.

Stagnation and demise are akin to the empires of yesteryear.[15] This is seen with many football managers who adopt the same approach in a different club (even with better players), but with less successful outcomes.

Succession planning or building leadership capacity is also at risk in the absence of a growth mindset. What we see in many schools is a 'cloned mindset' which is common in any sector with a master and apprentice model of leadership, which schools as well as many other professions still suffer from. What they may call a 'growth mindset' is actually growth in the image of the master (line manager), which then solidifies as a fixed mindset.

Learn every day. Have that as your intention the moment you commence your working day. Be observant and attentive in the present (rather than your eyes fixed to a device). When you least expect it, a moment of inspiration, original thought, or a better way to do something appears.

Yet before such a positive growing approach can take place, look back at how teachers have been 'moulded'. Teachers are a consequence of two major factors. Their own experience as a pupil and their teacher training during Initial Teacher Training (ITT) or more so their experiences and mentoring during their induction year as a Newly Qualified Teacher (NQT). With a great mentor they will more than likely have a strong foundation to be a great teacher.

Having the opposite risks an inconsistent and ambiguous basis by which to continue in the teaching profession. Therefore, cynicism can easily take hold and a reticence towards any new change in policy, training initiative or adopting a reflective practice. That said, a value-driven trainee teacher who has a growth mindset, who is ethical, honest and has integrity can overcome the issue of a poor mentor.

You can still go on to become a good or even great teacher despite having had negativity imposed on you by your mentor or line manager. You learn how not to seek their 'advice' which is often laden with shortcuts and do the bare minimum and blaming the students, the parents or the management but seldom taking responsibility for their own actions. In one way, you learn how 'not to do it' and you adopt a different approach and find inspiration from other colleagues who share good practice.

As a school leader, you have also been influenced by previous line managers and school leaders along the way. As I mentioned in my Preface, the many who helped shape me for the better. Just as much as I wanted to follow in the footsteps of the great and the good, I also learned how not to do things if the person leading the school or initiative is selfish, uninspiring, unethical, or lacking authenticity.

This is something which has shaped my career especially in the last decade where I learned to work around such inadequate school leaders and inept staff who have made the headlines for all the wrong reasons and ruined the careers of many staff and the life chances of hundreds of children, sadly.

A 'can do, want to (learn)' attitude is needed and not only is it needed to be demonstrated by you as a leader, you should find the staff who are also enthusiastic in finding new ways to address old issues. You as a leader can inspire growth by enabling mechanisms to exist in the school for staff to flourish. Often this is via promotion, but where there is a cap i.e. you have a team of effective subject leaders, then enable other high performers to lead cross-curricular teams to share good practice and innovate further.

This will allow those highly able staff to share elements of their practice to a wider audience. It also allows motivated staff to feel valued and further have a sense of belonging and commitment to the school and organisation, rather than feeling the need to look elsewhere and leave the school. That said, be gracious in enabling talented staff to move on if all avenues of opportunity have been exhausted in your school.

Governors

The further you ascend the leadership scale, the more likely you are to interact with Governors directly. They range from parent governors with a subconscious bias in the year group(s) that their child(ren) is/are in through to retired citizens, smiling and approving anything you say and even falling asleep in meetings. More cynical ones are those who feel they are inspectors, as in school inspectors or even Police inspectors, in their blunt suspicious approach to questioning and doubting the narrative presented by school leaders and then there are those Governors who feel they are a co-headteacher and want to do ad hoc lesson observations!

Whoever they are, again, knowing the intended outcome is key. It is highly political and especially as a Headteacher or Principal you may have to compromise on certain occasions, but as a mentor once said to me, "ask for double, if you get half then you have received what you had intended!"

Most governors do mean well and want the school to succeed with you as part of the SLT or as Headteacher or Principal. However, getting to know them, their preferences and their invariable biases will help you in having a more constructive dialogue than one which will be always trying to prove why or convince them etc. As a leadership coach once said to me to avoid these 'mind traps' that arise from 'above'. **I believe the greatest skill for a school leader and the most difficult to fully develop is to 'manage upwards' in a consistent manner.**

You may have the misfortune which I have had on many occasions especially in school leadership, of having to deal with either ignorance or arrogance (or worse both) in those having authority over you. Pause for a while and think about this in your career to date. . . It could be a less qualified, inexperienced or incompetent line manager. As school leaders, it could be Governors and Directors who really think they know better (but are not qualified teachers or have never taught in a classroom) when they are relying on opinions, whims and have little basis other than they can say what they want with no reproach. If they dither or delay and make errors, the blame is easily pointed to you as a school leader to become the scapegoat.

For example, I recall an e-mail sent by a Governor, when I was Principal. It was laden with erroneous statements and supposition forming a 'factual judgement' from the Board. My urge to reply immediately to set the record straight led me to add 'more fuel to the fire'. The Governor was already critical of an aspect of teaching and learning and despite me implying that the governor was not qualified to make such a judgement (having never been a teacher even though I felt the Governor was acting like an inspector).

By replying in a lengthy e-mail, it led to bitter recriminations several months later and the Board of Governors got their way, even if what I said was correct. How and when I said it may have allowed me to (think that I) had 'won the battle' or at least have a stalemate, but I 'lost the war' further on.

In such circumstances, it is disappointing that the school leadership is in (almost constant) conflict with an unsupportive, interfering, incompetent, or undermining Board. Such power struggles risk diminishing opportunities for children and staff. Avoid such confrontation even via the keyboard, as it often becomes entrenched and ignorance in authority will always dominate sadly.

Letting time pass and arranging to have a meeting, is something I would have benefited from over the years. In the instant messaging era and e-mails on your phones, although I advocate against having work e-mails on your phone as it is too easy for an instant reply. (Refer to Chapter E.)

A suggestion is to acknowledge the e-mail but allow time for a reply.

'Thank you for your e-mail, I will get back to you later in the week' ensures the 'status' (and ego) of the Governor has been respected, but it allows you important thinking time before a decision, or a formal response is provided.

Governors can also be less engaging. Whilst this sounds great, as a school leader you do not want everything rubber-stamped by a passive Governing Board. Instead, you do need a critical friend to help shape your thinking and of course hold you to account.

If you have the rare opportunity to shape the Board dynamics, then have individuals who may be experts in their own field, but collectively provide a broad skillset on the Board i.e. finance, legal, medical, parent, community. Yet also have a recently retired school leader or serving Headteacher (if they can spare the time) to be a committed Governor with a qualified and experienced eye and view of your core function as a school: learning and teaching.

H

Humility

You may be craving for your name on the door of your office, or the reserved car parking slot, but really school leadership is a position of great trust and responsibility as much as it is a great privilege.

Leadership is not for everyone nor is it meant to be. It is not an easy decision to step up. If it was an easy decision for you, be careful to consider your motivations for assuming the role. Sometimes ambition gets in the way of ability and the ineffective leaders are soon exposed or they quickly move on to a new school with the same ineffective bluff they used in their old school to get by before moving on again (and again) when found out. Furthermore, when facing the end of a leadership tenure, if you feel you have tried your best or fulfilled as much as you had hoped for, it is not an easy decision to step aside or 'down' from your role or move out.

A sense of servant leadership will enable you to reaffirm your purpose of 'being there for others'. With this, qualities of compassion and consideration will enamour all who interact with you. As you establish yourself as a leader, there is a risk of complacency in practice. You may have devised a 'winning formula', that generates well-deserved success, but there is also a risk of taking others for granted.

As you grow further in the role, along with possible social media presence, the personality can become more important than the person. You have now been called an 'expert'. Often you rehash the same topic and presentation a dozen times over at various conferences and seminars. Within 18 months, the issues you are presenting time and time again become outmoded or less relevant.

The same can be said when your profile is shared with the speakers list, with accolades of leading 'outstanding' schools (but this was more than five years ago). This could risk promoting past (rightfully earned) glories but could lead to a diminished value of what you are presenting.

Is what you are presenting the current expert view? Or rather is it an excellent strategy that worked in your school several years ago?

A sense of gratitude and being grateful to others will remind you of the staff upon whose shoulders is the leader carried. An example is to give credit and acknowledge those who make things happen for you as a leader. I presented a technology transformation journey to dozens of school leaders, but I was keen to acknowledge my thanks to the admin team, data manager and the exams officer by name. Public recognition by displaying their names in the presentation. (It was deliberately not the last slide of presentation as it could be on par with the end of movie credits in the cinema, where many do not pay attention and walk out!) It was also intentional to remind school leaders in the audience that success is down to teamwork and it takes several others to make a project successful.

Humility will carry you far in your personal qualities. (Being haughty will grab the attention of others but will be short-lived.) Of course, it can be seen as a paradox where school leaders are expected to be at the forefront, facing challenges and being bold and daring. Yet with a sense of humility coupled with gratitude, it will enable you to carry staff with you in times of crisis and enable you to provide effective stewardship.

A way to ensure this is a culture in the school is to have a charitable and philanthropic pillar which makes it incumbent on everyone in the school to help others and if an external project, to spread awareness, volunteer time and if needed raise money for the good cause that the school is endorsing. In an Executive Headship role where I led a Primary School and a Secondary school, I intentionally factored in one lesson a week, 1/40th dedicated to charity, a sense of giving and community service but also to support wellbeing.[16] The aim in the future was to have a blocked off timetable for the whole campus, so older children could read to younger children or help younger children with numeracy.

Also, the aim was to establish a true egalitarian workforce where site staff would also help in a charity project in the classroom. Thus, all staff are treated equally but to make it visible to students too and change perceptions and challenge any prejudice that the value of a someone cleaning the toilets is just as important (if not more) as the teacher in the classroom.

Hypocrisy

"Do as I say not as I do!" The excuse that annoying teacher from your childhood era would say. You expect students to apologise for being late to your lesson, but do you return the apology to students if you are late to their lesson? Or do you only apologise to your line manager's meetings as a matter of rank respect?

School leaders who are immersed in arrogance call it privilege (but they apply it as a perk), the earned right to flout expectations or norms for others. An example I recall was school leaders 'on duty' skipping the queue in the canteen to eat their lunch first and then 'patrol' the school site. However, when I was on duty, I used to wait until the end of lunch to eat and often it meant my 'first choice' meal was sold out, but it did not disappoint me as I was reassured that the children had eaten. (A book has been published on this exact theme, almost a decade after I used to practise this, but somehow, I do not think the author was inspired by me![17]) Yet from the staff body, whom you are leading, it falls foul and leaves a horrid perception of you. Students even see this and say, "Why is (Mr/Miss) so and so pushing in?" as they jump the queue with cries of "Sir/Miss, we were here before you!"

Indeed, I took this practice further, when I was involved in a charity project in West Africa, whereby I was the 'guest of honour' for a presentation and a meal. I caused a major stir when I insisted the driver eat before me and I waited to eat last. The hosts were offended as to why what they perceived to be a 'lower ranked' person was eating before me, but I held my ground in my usual stubborn self! (An awful and traumatic moment happened after the meal, when I witnessed some children from the streets who came to eat the leftovers. They were literally eating any rice they found on the ground of the venue, sifting to eat rice coated in soil or dirt. This has haunted me ever since and on a personal note, I have always ensured whenever I eat rice, I finish all the rice on my plate.)

Other aspects of hypocrisy appear with the inconsistent treatment or application of policy especially when applied to yourself/your peers. There is nothing worse than denying a staff member an early finish one day for a personal request, but you or your colleagues in the Senior Leadership Team (SLT), leave early, or arrive late as you 'were busy' (with the justification that you work late into the evening every day). This implies that your right to have flexible onsite hours is more important as you are busier. It implies that other staff are less important, or their 'busy' demand is less so. This is disingenuous. One rule for staff and one rule for leaders is flawed. It will produce short term results but over time, the culture of the school risks becoming toxic.

Another example I have seen is the 'reserved parking' slots in school car parks. I have even seen this for a Headteacher's PA, who has a reserved parking slot! Whilst I do not doubt the important role a PA holds in a school, by elevating the PA in the organisational hierarchy status and putting the PA on par with the SLT, it sends out a divisive message to the staff body (both teaching and admin staff). I would always prefer a 'first come, first served' basis.

Therefore, in my own experience when applying this principle, I have missed 'my parking slot' (where I usually park arriving early to work) whenever I arrived later than my 'usual' arrival time. This is a true meritocracy and it rewards those staff who arrive early to have the 'better' (closer to the entrance or exit) car parking slot than those who feel a sense of entitlement with their reserved slot despite arriving later or leaving earlier.

However, other factors will determine parking availability and also priority. These include the size of the school car park and the access to the school site (not all schools are purpose built in entirety in one build phase, but rather annexes are built over time taking over parts of the playing fields or the existing school car park). As a Headteacher or Principal you may need to attend meetings offsite and therefore need to access to your car during the day and have a spot to park upon your return often due to segued meetings, so there may be some valid justification for dedicated parking slots if the school car park is not so spacious!

Another recent example is that of the pandemic. Penalising staff for not wearing a mask or socially distancing in meetings, whilst you do not wear your mask in your office (when you are meeting staff around a table in close proximity) are noted by staff and colleagues as double standards. It lowers their respect for you and a lot of (well-earned) credibility could be lost in a week.

Be sure to hold yourself to account as a school leader in your own self-treatment. With additional 'power', (authority and responsibility) comes a greater scrutiny. Be your own harshest critic.

Humour

It may sound obvious, but many school leaders are wrapped up in being 'serious' school leaders who lack authenticity. (Refer to Chapter A.) This is because they feel the need to 'play a role of being a (school) leader' in a rehearsed, trained and conditioned manner rather than being a human and a leader of humans.

Children need to feel safe and happy. This provides a strong basis for achievement. However, you can have achievement by putting the fear of failure into students and limit risk-taking. This would result in high student exam outcomes but (hothoused) drained and unhappy students. The safety and happiness are found in the qualities of compassion and empathy but also humour. Having a sense of humour and seeing the funny side of various issues does bring about the human in you. This is important. It is not about being the court jester or the 'trying so hard to be funny' for the students will reply that you "are so not funny".

The seriousness of the role and the weight of responsibilities should not take away the great privilege to be a leader. However, the moody, grumpy, fault-picking self-importance or taking yourself too seriously, does not provide the security that children need in a school leader. It provides a function and a way to operate, but not much more than that.

It does also matter who the audience is. My tendency to be sarcastic to those who I do not respect (for their ignorance or arrogance) can lead to afterthoughts of jokes which I should not have said i.e. in front of Governors. Being witty and satirical can lead to a rapid apology moments later, but the damage could be too late to fix! Having a sense of humour rather than always being flippant or sarcastic is a lesson I should have learned earlier on in school leadership to avoid dozens of apologies afterwards!

Schools are organisations for children and teenagers, whose positive emotions and feelings are built on a bedrock of thinking, dreaming, believing, as well as laughing. Be generous and charitable in your smile, warmth and care. Another aspect of humour is that it helps support your own wellbeing and reduces stress levels. By laughing and smiling you are removing tension from your own body. The physiological and psychological benefits and positive emotional wellbeing of having a sense of humour in the working day cannot be overstated. It allows you to deal with the unexpected, the irrational or the absurd and take it in your stride.

I

Inspection

In England as elsewhere globally, schools are amongst the most regulated sectors in government. Invariably the inspection of quality and standards, whether this is teaching and learning, outcomes, safety or leadership and management, will lead to that 'public listing' of your performance as the school leadership.

As a Principal or Headteacher it is very personal as your name is on the report. There is no other sector where an 'official seal' of approval or disapproval is so publicly displayed. Parents and staff (usually from other schools) form their opinions about whether the school is a 'good' school or a failing school. Suffice to say, who would want to be a Headteacher!

Two or three days could literally undo a Headteacher's career built up over two or three decades. Is this just? Often it is disproportionate and stacked against the schools in challenging circumstances. In England, this could be a catchment with high levels of deprivation[18] or in the international school context with schools who have lower fees (compared to more expensive schools in the city, who by default attract the better qualified and experienced staff due to higher salaries and have better facilities).

Such leaders of these schools will always persevere against all odds, sailing against the tide on lonely paths and post-inspection can face the wrath of the Board as being the ones who are made to be scapegoats and consequently their legacy is tarnished. Whereas leaders of schools (in England) which are not striving for excellence but do enough to get by, also known as 'coasting' schools,[19] seem to 'survive' the inspection, a bit like the football managers who manage 5 or 6 clubs in a decade with no silverware.

Of course, schools need to be held to account. The challenge for you as a school leader is how to ensure you have enough evidence for the inspection framework criteria, without compromising your philosophy and beliefs of education, learning and teaching. I say this as most inspection frameworks are to serve the agenda of the Government in authority at that time rather than to help improve the education sector.

This is difficult as some areas of compromise will be needed, but if it stifles growth, innovation and inspiration then ensure it is only a temporary diversion for the sake of the inspection rather than a permanent culture shift to become a school which prioritises inspections.

I recall an example, when I was Principal, where I was having an 'agree to disagree' moment with the lead inspector, who could not fully understand child-led learning. The staff were very privileged to have had six months of preparation from a Finnish instructor and had managed to establish learning stations in Key Stage 1.

However, the lead inspector was unable to appreciate that there were multiple learning stations with some learning mathematics, others having an English writing session whilst other children reading, and others learning science, all running concurrently. The inspector kept saying "it says, mathematics on the timetable, but only a few students are learning mathematics". I did explain that the inspection framework set out expectations of timetable allocation per 'subject' and I would rather have a cross-curricular theme across each morning in Key Stage 1, but it was not permitted as per that inspection framework.

I had to then co-observe with her for consecutive lessons to show that all students would indeed cover reading, writing and mathematics on a rotation based on the individual child's needs. Some may need more time and focus on mathematics and others may need more support with reading; so, it would not simply be 1 hour of mathematics, 1 hour of reading and 1 hour of writing each morning for all students at the same time.

The issue was akin to being too future focused and the current people (inspection team) being out of touch. This reminded me of the quote from the film 'Back to the Future' when the main protagonist, Marty

McFly said "I guess you guys aren't ready for that yet. But your kids are gonna love it".[20] I was then told it is "not worth challenging inspectors, because in the end you would not win!"

Now this is not a rebuttal against having long-retired practitioners, academics or civil servants as inspectors. However, it provides more credibility to have serving practitioners as inspectors whether this is in the UK or internationally. In my example, the inspector had not been working in or leading schools for more than fifteen years. She qualified in the 1960s, but inspecting a school in the late 2010s, it is easy to appreciate the disconnect and gap of working curriculum knowledge and the innovation that has taken place especially in Primary education.

I recall another inspector once, telling me that our school "needs to have more computers in the classroom" when he could not understand that laptops and tablets were also ICT. It must also be noted that, he also last worked in schools nearly twenty years ago. ICT has also changed even more rapidly than the curriculum in that time!

Lessons I learned with the benefit of hindsight are many. If I had prepared a policy for this curriculum modification and the rationale behind it and defined the technology shift from a physical PC at the back or side of the classroom to devices, it may have helped shape the inspectors' understanding just as much as it helped support the understanding of other stakeholders such as Governors who are retired and have perhaps not been in a school setting for decades too!

The insecure school leader thinks the inspection is the only aim of proving they are a successful leader. Indeed, such leaders are even rather disingenuous in saying they "do not care about what the inspectors say," whilst they prep for an inspection, months in advance. These are the same school leaders who complain about inspections but are the first to boast a positive inspection report on the school website, on the school gate and on social media!

I am a firm believer that you as a school leader can achieve great outcomes for children by doing what is right for students. That said, having the skill to focus and prioritise and where needed to 'jump through hoops' is a necessary if not annoying expectation.

Interview

As a school leader, it is fair to assume you are adept in attending and being successful in interviews. It may have taken several attempts, applications, hopes raised and dashed thinking if you were shortlisted or even more emotional if you were shortlisted and called for interview; and then to be told you were not successful at interview.

Now in your role, you are 'on the other side of the desk': You will either be on the interview panel, a chair of a panel or the hiring manager/senior recruiter. Be sincere in interviewing all candidates. If they have been shortlisted for interview, then they meet the criteria for the job and it should be down to the interview and performance on any other tasks i.e. a lesson observation if a teacher or data task if an admin role, to see if they are successful.

I have had the misfortune to have worked alongside some colleagues who have foregone conclusions of some candidates prior to interview. This is wholly unacceptable. Such prejudice and collusion show it was not a level playing field and certainly not an equal opportunities employer no matter how much the school (leader) may boast of 'investing in people'. If the candidate is 'weak' (on paper) but is still called for interview, this reflects very badly on inadequate human resources (HR) systems.

I have had the highs and lows of career progression over the past two decades of successful applications, interviews and job offers but also of having been rejected for various roles that I applied for. The reasons given for not being successful are quite staggering at times. Examples include a lack of experience or conversely, I have too much leadership experience for a teaching role, or I am overqualified for the intended role.

(It is difficult having been a Principal or Headteacher, to apply for roles other than Principal/Vice Principal, Head or Deputy Head as often schools do not 'believe' you would want a teaching role or settle for what they think is a demotion or 'lower' role for you). However, surely either of these would have been picked up in the application form/CV? Therefore, why shortlist for interview in the first instance?

Only two headteachers had the professional courtesy to offer what I call sincere feedback. In a middle leadership (subject leader) role that I applied for, one Headteacher mentioned that I showed how I would provide challenge for the higher achievers, but I did not discuss enough on supporting the students who were lower attainers.

Another headteacher provided feedback from an interview for an SLT role and mentioned how I focused a lot on new systems and enhancing existing systems, but I did not focus enough on staff development. Valuable insight to help shape my teaching and leadership outlook in the following decade to come.

Either way I respected these two headteachers as they made an effort to provide me with feedback on the same day rather than expect HR to update me after a few days. This often means there is no formal follow-up and you have to chase HR to confirm what you have been dreading "thank you for your e-mail. Unfortunately, you were not successful. We wish you all the best for your future applications". (Or worse no reply whatsoever.)

There is also the lazy or insincere school leader who hides behind the veneer of professional bureaucracy and does not offer feedback or ignores an e-mail, despite saying at the end of the interview, "we will be in touch in the coming days". As a school leader, have the courtesy and dignity to offer feedback in a timely manner. I would suggest within 2 working days is reasonable. I would also say by having effective weighted criteria scoring for each stage of the interview/assessment, you should be able to provide feedback on the same day, in person preferably.

Ask questions as per an agreed framework. It is even better to add weighting and a scoring system to measure responses and maintain objectivity. This is then consistent for all candidates. Of course, there may be a follow-up based on their response, but it ensures equity of treatment. The feedback and evaluation, which should be agreed upon by yourself and your peers on the panel, also becomes fair and transparent with a weighting system which maintains objectivity as opposed to a casual informal opinion, which is laden with bias and lacks impartiality.

Often, I have faced some ridiculous questions in interview. "Why do you want to work at this school?" or "Why have you applied for this role?" Well, if you had read my application, I have mentioned half a dozen reasons there! The better interviewers pick up content from your application form and refers to it in the interview. Even if the candidate is not successful it shows quality, care and due diligence. It also shows respect and professional courtesy for the effort made to complete an application form and write a statement/letter of application.

Another challenge you will face is how to maintain objectivity if there are both internal and external candidates. This can be done as mentioned previously with a fair weighting and scoring mechanism rather than an 'opinion' formed on the day. If the latter, by default, knowing the internal candidate, it will no doubt impair objectivity. I also recommend that the process is explained to all candidates, from the outset, that it is a weighted or objective scoring methodology for all candidates to avoid any bitter recrimination if the internal candidate was not successful.

Interviews can often expose internal politics of a school as well. As a school leader, ensure this never happens. It is sloppy, weak and can detrimentally affect the reputation of the few individuals of the school or even the school itself as a place of nepotism, bias and unfairness. Lesson observations can expose this clearly. An attempt to sully the candidate saying it was not a successful lesson as "progress by the students was not being made" is an easy one to put across without substantiating your claim.

Do not allow yourself or your panel members merely to go through the motions and fob off a candidate and feign interest in how they are responding in interview. Certainly, do not give a reason for rejection at interview that the candidate does not have enough experience or qualifications (as this should have been picked up during shortlisting).

To shortlist for interview, it should be about 'what' the candidate can bring to the school/organisation, having reviewed their experience and qualifications. During the interview you learn about 'who' the candidate is. Unfortunately, in many appointments, there is too much nepotism and it is 'who' the candidate knows (high up in the school organisation) and not what the candidate knows. The 'what' they known or can bring to the organisation, comes up in the informal interview before being appointed (as a foregone conclusion).

Intelligence

This may sound obvious. Leaders need to be intelligent as opposed to thinking they are clever! By default, the neurodiversity implies some people are better at cognitive processing, cognitive loading and cognitive ability; but with the appropriate effort and practice, skills can be developed and enhanced. This applies to you as school leaders but also to your community of students and staff.

With effort and the appropriate framework of provision, every child can succeed, every staff member can flourish and every school can thrive. Hard work with honesty, will always prove to be superior to the opposite: Lazy liars! School leaders need to uphold this belief. Effort with resilience can make all the difference between crossing the threshold or having the benefit of hindsight regret that "I wish I could have prepared more".

Put this in the context of between five and seven years of secondary education with six years of primary education previously. How is it standards and outcomes are so low for a large proportion of students? Of course, the challenging situations of children from dysfunctional or less supportive households will prove to be major barriers to success.

However, most students go to school with the hope of some level of success to be 'educated' (and obtain meaningful qualifications). Contextualise this further and consider the example of a 'core subject' in Secondary school. (This term is rather derogatory as it negates the value of other subjects and devalues the whole curriculum.) Consider my own subject training, mathematics. Allow us to make the following assumptions:

- At least 3.5 hours a week of lessons in this subject.
- Four full years (35 weeks) of teaching (Year 7 to Year 10).
- Half-academic year of teaching in Year 11 i.e. finish teaching by half-term of the second term.
- A 'pass' at an exam is at 50% (though I have my own views about written exams[21]). This assumption is based on a 'pass' at a master's degree, or a lower second division degree. (Though the % for Grade 5 in GCSE a Grade C for AS/A level varies per exam subject and exam board.)

Why is it that over 11 years of formal education, ALL students cannot obtain at least 50%? This is a challenge I put to all school leaders as well as myself and what has kept me awake on many occasions. It is a genuine national (and international) disgrace.

Doing the calculations (excuse the awful teacher pun!) and we have the following: 3.5 x 35 school weeks x 4.5 school years = 551.25 hours of mathematical learning. Yet the fact that more than a third of students in Year 11 fail to achieve this 'pass' threshold (which is often below 50%) should be sounding alarm bells for all school leaders.

This is systemic failure and I have even heard former Headteachers boast "I was never any good at maths," or, "I too failed maths the first time (of sitting the exam)". You would never boast about failing English or having poor literacy but boasting about being weak at mathematics or being less numerate seems to be a badge of honour (rather than shame).

Yet effort should not only be there to do enough to get the minimum but rather effort should push towards excellence. The now famous '10,000 hours to mastery'[22] can be analysed further in the context of work:

Use the basis of a 40-hour working week. Then 10,000 hours is the same as 250 working weeks, or a little over 5 years of dedication (assuming a few weeks off for holiday, rest and recuperation). Effort-based intelligence provides a mindset to overcome a struggle and recover from a setback and also develop better memory skills.[23]

J

Justice

Leadership is not solely about doing, enacting policy, or giving direction but rather there must be a sense of justice. As leaders of schools, you need to ensure excellence in provision and outcomes for your students in your care as well as levelling the playing field elsewhere.

Similarly in staff recruitment, promotion and retention, opportunities should be based on merit. During the past few years, organisations, sectors and institutions have had to reflect on their structures and representation. Schools also have begun to show much more consideration on matters such as inclusion, diversity, equity and anti-racism, to help ensure leadership reflects the school community and/or provides role models for the students to aspire towards in gauging that authority is not in the mould of one strata of society.

School leaders who live with care and respect as key tenets of their practice will ensure this levelling happens within their school but be an advocate for it to happen in other schools and in society also. The leaders who are true pillars of education speak for others and do not perceive them as competition, but what they want for others is what they want for themselves. Whereas the colonising leaders simply pack up and leave a school and take their team with them wherever they go.

An example to enable justice is to have effective communication within the community by giving a voice to all key stakeholders.[24] The bigger challenge as a school leader is to be the voice for the voiceless. This is not liking the sound of our own voice nor for vanity purposes of self-promotion (on social media), but to speak for just causes.

Education is very political. Policy makers from governments have their agenda and views on what they perceive a successful education is. Employers and Universities also have their expectations on how school leavers should be qualified and ready for life beyond school. Depending on your jurisdiction you could be competing in the for-profit international schools or struggling with public funding challenges on a national level.

To further exasperate the geo-political context, the changes in the world especially during the COVID-19 pandemic has exposed the technological challenges in schools. This has left millions of children on the 'wrong side' of the digital divide with digital poverty prevalent.[25] Calls for digital inclusion have amplified with school leaders campaigning for additional laptops and tablets to support the vulnerable students left out.

Other socio-political issues such as discrimination 'outside' of school, in the community, in the workplace limit life chances for school leavers despite having some academic qualifications or education 'success'. All of which amounts to a cry for equity and social justice. (Refer to Chapter E.)

As a school leader you need to ensure justice for your community. Provide opportunities for your staff to grow and share the platform with other schools and as much do so for your students to interact and collaborate with projects and other school communities. A challenge to consider in terms of 'future focus' is how do you follow up and offer support for your school leavers in terms of how they fare in the academic world at university or in the world of work?

An interesting model I once saw during a visit to a Charter School in the Bronx, New York, was the flags of each college (university) of former students who attended these colleges. A silver frame, if they had enrolled and a gold frame if they had successfully graduated (to measure the attrition/dropout rate of their school alumni). This school also provided mentoring for their former school students on the college campus to provide further study skills support to enable them to successfully graduate with a degree. Their belief was that social justice can only be attained with children from poverty graduating from college (university).

Of course, context is key, university is not meant to be mandatory for all people, it is a valid aspiration and an opportunity afford for all. The key is to have an excellent Primary and Secondary education, from which the young adults can make informed choices of whether they want to study for a degree immediately (or later in adult, working life) or whether they want to have the means to have a fulfilled career, vocation and employment elsewhere without having had to have studied at university.

Juggle

Few can throw and catch three balls in an ongoing loop and thus juggle, but the role of a school leader . . . or let us go back to the start of your career; the role of the teacher, is to be in almost perpetual multitasking in the school day. Other adults outside of education think it is 'an easy job' with some teaching from a book and students copying and learning and long holidays. How naïve is such a held view?!

The closest preparation you may have had was in an interview setting to have the 'in-tray' exercise to prioritise actions and tasks. I recall stumbling on one such activity in an interview assessment, where my default instinct ranked as first importance a safeguarding concern reported to me in my 'role' as the Headteacher.

The actual 'answer' was the blocked toilets as the priority. This meant no toilets were functioning in the school and this immediate health and safety risk meant the school risked being closed for the day until it was resolved.

(I would say though with hindsight, if the safeguarding risk is immediate, it must take priority. My inexperience at that time showed as it was a reported concern, which would be delegated to the Designated Safeguarding Lead, rather than me having to deal with it immediately.)

Specific examples of in-tray tasks have included the following:

- Health & safety issue: Ceiling collapsed in a corridor.
- Safeguarding allegation against a staff member.

- Angry parents arrived in the school office demanding to see you.
- Medical issue: Child injured and an ambulance has been called.
- Flooded science laboratory.
- Multiple teacher absence, not enough teachers for each class.
- No internet in the IT suite.
- Heating (or air conditioning if the school is in a hot climate) failed.

It is just as vital about knowing who to delegate to as it is to juggle with what you can see to or resolve in your own capacity.

Another activity used to assess prioritising, as seen in recent years, is the 'Diamond 9' model[26] to organise your own thinking and perceptions of priorities on a theme (where you are given 10 or 12 choices and have to 'shortlist' and prioritise to 9).

Most important			X		
		X		X	
	X		X		X
		X		X	
Least important			X		

Choose 9 and place the most important on top, followed by the next two and then three in the middle, with two below and the least important below this (with some factors deemed completely irrelevant and not even appearing on the diamond).

For example, which factors are the most important for student progress? Choose from: school leadership, teachers, parents, student friendships, assessments, planning, emotional wellbeing, technology, planning, timetable, school building, revision.

There are no right answers in this model, but can you justify your selection. The task evaluates your ability to present an argument for or against as well as your leadership judgement.

The scale of multi-tasking as a teacher is immense notwithstanding the various out of classroom tasks such as planning, feedback on students' work, data entry or analysis, parent communication and responding to e-mails from staff too. The role the teacher must take on in the classroom can often be seen in multiple roles during the lesson on a responsive basis or even reactive approach:

- Teacher
- Facilitator
- Supervisor
- Mentor
- Coach
- And even Entertainer

For a school leader, this becomes more 'scaled up' as you need to consider other stakeholders. You may still teach but as you are managing staff who teach or support learning, this ability to manage workload and how you deal with staff who have their own unique personality and professional competence will be a challenge that you need to develop in your role.

You will still supervise students on 'duties' but also essentially you are 'supervising staff' to ensure they are on duty as per the rota to help provide safe supervision of students. You will mentor and coach staff more than perhaps students. Whilst you may not be entertaining, you will need to have charisma and inspire staff in your role.

Yet you will also need to juggle the demands from external stakeholders such as other schools, local authorities, government departments, multi-agency liaison.

Being versatile is as much within your personality as it is something that can be learned. Most people prefer being in their comfort zone and follow an expected schedule of tasks, events that they can prepare and deliver to a high standard. This is very reasonable. Examples I mentioned here are more on how you respond in times of crisis management.

Yet the immense workload means you cannot assume it will end at some point. Even as term ends, the planning for next term/year continues. You need to be able to compartmentalise time in the day and week to ensure completion. New school leaders often take on a lot and commence or initiate many tasks or projects, but the mistake is to stay back after hours to finish off tasks which were partly completed earlier in the day/week.

The advice is to ensure what you intend to start has an allocated time for completion. It could result in being selfish (in the short term) and have a 'one theme' day to ensure the school improvement plan is finished or the data analysis for the Governors is ready and then juggle the other tasks and prioritise around this.

Joy

Happiness, celebrating achievements, a sense of contentment and fulfilment. There is no better feeling than knowing you have added tremendous value to a child's life and their outlook going forward or that you have enabled a staff member to grow and further progress in their career.

Enabling staff to lay the blueprint for students to aim for success and fulfil their aspirations and ambitions is something that you can take a rightful sense of pride and purpose in. Asides from the 'results' day (usually in August) where students, as young adults leave the school to commence 'adulthood' either at university or in the world of work, the joy of parents and staff also resonate.

When applying this in the staff context, grow staff as better practitioners and in many cases as future leaders. Whether this is in curriculum or pastoral areas, promotions to middle leadership, whole cohort responsibilities or supporting their journey to senior school leadership, it does provide a great sense of joy. The happiness in their career progression should be cause for you to share in the celebration.

Where success did not materialise, the inevitable tears of sadness will appear i.e. not achieving expected exam results. However, with swift intervention and robust support, the 'if at first you don't succeed, try again' approach is needed. This resilience allows the student to bounce back but also it could be argued that the joy, coupled with relief can be even stronger with this feeling of achievement, having not been so successful first time around.

Despite all the negative press, challenges and stress, know that under your great leadership, students and staff are thriving and parents are immensely grateful.

From your perspective, it is too easy to be merely relieved a term has ended or the school inspection is over. Reach for the warmth and share the joy with everyone who matters; both within the school and in your personal lives too.

K

Kettle

As someone who has never drunk tea or coffee in any school, I am the worst to explain this, but it is vital to have a break. Put on the kettle, have a break. Make a cup of tea or coffee. Spend time away from your office or workspace.

Have a break with staff on an informal 15-20 minutes a day. Buy them a coffee! (In the canteen, rather than in the staff room. As a school leader, let the staff room be for staff to have their private sounding off space. They may even have a gripe about your decisions (even if it is for the greater good of the school or for the benefit of the students), but it is their right to have that space to express themselves with peers.

The walk out of your workspace will bring oxygen to the brain, but also remind you of your purpose as a school leader. Watch learning in lessons, across the curriculum, from practical lessons to creative lessons and the moment of understanding that lights up a child's face of having understood something new! Chat with teachers as they prepare and plan for resources to further enhance student learning experiences and the informal conversations with other staff asking how they are doing? Compare 'notes' with colleagues on your favourite football team, other sports or hobbies or a recent book you have read or film you have seen.

In this increasingly digital and technological era, the long uninterrupted hours spent in front of a screen risks serious longer term eyesight damage. Consider the 20-20-20 rule[27] which should be applied to the whole school community as well as yourself. This is to have a break from the screen and prevent or reduce digital eye strain every 20 minutes for at least 20 seconds by looking away at something 20 feet away, which is essentially across the classroom. (A bias towards the UK imperial length. 20ft which is just over 6m, but 20-20-6 does not read as well!)

Furthermore, our mobile phone 'addiction' of having to pick it up, check or respond to notifications and scan or skim through 'updates' on various feeds be it news or social media has led to a generation unable to communicate face to face effectively. How often do you find two adults in a restaurant on their mobiles rather than having a pleasant face to face conversation? If more than two, how often do you see the other person not in the conversation, turn to their phone for solace!

Have a regular break from devices. Consider a 'phone-free Friday' or at least a day every weekend where you are away from your phone, social media and even streaming on your TV.

Emerging from the various COVID-19 lockdowns across the world, it has been reassuring that the value of human connection (in the physical world as opposed to virtual world) has reignited. Use this as momentum to have less time on screens but make it a work habit in school.

We have themes such as DEAR (Drop Everything And Read), why not have an offline hour a week in school too. This will allow the whole community to reconnect and value human company rather than the anxiety from the virtual world (expectations of likes, comments and updates from various social media channels).

Kind

It sounds rather obvious and even daft to mention it in this book, but how many line managers are unkind, rude, blunt, or standoffish? Being kind is not that difficult! Not only will it keep your stress levels down, but more often than not, it will resonate amongst staff, students and parents to reciprocate kindness, warmth and be more receptive to what you are communicating and meet your expectations.

Kind and caring go hand in hand, but the corporate care i.e. results driven takes away the human side of you as a leader. The 'fake' (social) media smile or conversation results in students or staff not valuing anything (from the leadership) unless they feel a sense of mutual benefit. It becomes a case of "what's in it for me?"

Kindness can be taught as much as it is innate. If you look at children in early infants, they will play together with no issues whatsoever. The snatching and "this is mine" comments come from children witnessing or imitating selfishness (at home or school) and they too develop this trait.

The question for you to reflect on is what do you care about? Being kind, caring and considerate will make the school culture something truly exceptional. The benefits of inclusion and tolerance and the strength in diversity will produce students who are genuine leaders of tomorrow. Many schools say their students are future leaders, but is it rather their students are successful academically and able to enter a leading university and subsequently a profession?

To have future leaders who are genuine and not robotic or rehearsed starts by being kind and caring and then increasing your awareness around you. These will no doubt lead to opinionated and even politically active students, i.e. they care about issues elsewhere just as much as (or more than) their own social life (popularity online or weekend entertainment).

Transfer this principle to staff and ask them the same question. What do they care about? A kind workforce will care about more than ensuring the students 'do well in exams' in their department. They will care about the school in its entirety. They challenge any negative behaviour shown by students anywhere in the school, rather than hurry down the corridor to get to their lesson or use part of their 'non-contact' (non-teaching) period to challenge any tardiness in students moving from one classroom to the next.

Whereas staff who are not so committed to the collective responsibility of the school community, walk past such students who are late to lessons without challenging them. Such staff are more concerned that it is their 'free' period and do not want to 'waste' part of this time in doing someone else's job (as they assume it the role of the pastoral, behavioural support team's role to look at attendance and punctuality).

In short, be kind and want success for others as you would for yourself.

Keep

Hoarding, as some of my family may say to me I do so well, can be seen as a bad habit. (I still have a book from my primary school and most of my exercise books from my secondary school).

Of course, in this era of consideration to the planet and the environment, reduce, reuse, recycle are all responsible traits and keeping things that can be used elsewhere by someone else is irresponsible. Though I am not sure who would want my exercise book from when I was 13 years old?!

Keeping certain 'memories' (thank you gifts, cards etc.) for posterity and nostalgia will potentially help your emotional wellbeing. However, do keep a record of your achievements and of your failings and file it as reflections. This can be in the form of a diary, a few typed notes but make a point of having it elsewhere than in your mind and memory. By having something to read, it will help internalise your thinking and support your leadership and professional development. (I know this is rather contradictory, avoid remembering something to help your mind think?!) This approach also acts as a reference point for any future decision-making to avoid déjà-vu (negative) outcomes.

In terms of keeping, it can also be for inspiration as much as it is for your own personal reflection on an achievement, for example. With the use of the smartphone, you can easily capture an image, a sign, some great learning, or resource in an instant.

The term 'magpie' was introduced to me more than a decade ago. As per the dictionary definition: "someone who likes to collect many different types of objects".[28] Taking inspiration and blatantly copying other schools in some instances was encouraged (under the guise of sharing or should I say taking good practice)!

However, in your journey of school leadership, keep anything you find useful along the way. This is definitely true in the first 100 days in your tenure but also whenever you have the opportunity to visit other schools, other 'venues' (tradeshows, conferences etc.) or in discussions with staff, parents and students, type a note, record a voice comment of a quote, take a photo of something inspiring or produce a file as a reference i.e. this could be a presentation, a summary document, a spreadsheet analysis of key facts and figures.

Now you do not have to be as pedantic as me and back up your files over the years by school, by headings and by year, but this archiving mindset will help you a lot in indexing your kept inspiration, memories and evidence in an almost portfolio manner. (Refer to Chapter Y.)

L

Listen

Many school leaders talk a lot, write a lot. Yet if they do appear to be listening, it is because they are waiting to speak rather than paying attention to what is being said. However, the more effective school leaders are more attentive to the person or audience in front of them. Active listening is a great skill but one that needs developing in many people, especially leaders who until now may have only listened to the sound of their own voice! It starts by engaging with others in the present, here and now.

Paying attention is increasingly difficult in this era, where attention spans (online) have become shorter and shorter with the option to 'Skip Ads' or 'Skip Intro' for online videos. Yet to have the professional courtesy to listen to the person speaking with you, without interrupting (something sadly I keep falling foul of) is something worth training yourself and developing these effective communication skills. Make the effort to ask questions following what has been said, which will at least provide some assurance to the recipient that you have paid attention to what they have said.

Avoid the insincerity that some teachers demonstrate. The teacher asks the class, how their school holidays were to reciprocate and interject with the boast of how great the teacher's holiday was and where they went etc. (This is also quite offensive in some school contexts, of lower socio-economic households. The teacher tells the class where they went to some expensive and exotic location, whilst most of the children may not have had a holiday at all). A classic example of not only liking the sound of your own voice coupled with waiting to speak but even seeking affirmation for what you are saying to the 'captive' audience.

You learn a lot by listening and more importantly taking an active interest shows you care and value the staff, students, parents etc. This social capital becomes vital as great leadership generates followship. Building care and trust will help you lead the team and/or organisation to a greater level and reach new heights in further raising standards.

In other areas of your role, you find school leaders showing tremendous discourtesy and poor etiquette. How many times do we find leaders typing emails on their devices during presentations or contributions from other colleagues? This models arrogance (and if unintended then it shows ignorance), or less importance of others and it is unacceptable. You are better off leaving the room of the presentation or conference to tend to your e-mails rather than 'feign interest' by pretending to focus or doing so intermittently whilst on your device.

I have been in such situations more from ignorance than arrogance I hasten to add! I thought I was multi-tasking when e-mailing during meetings and presentations, but in fact it is disrespectful. If anything, it taught me to have a meeting agenda to be purposeful for the all attendees rather than colleagues queuing up to present. (Refer to Chapter A.)

Be in the present and respect the person you are meeting/talking with and to never answer the phone if it rings as it devalues the presence of the person you are speaking with.[29] Ask yourself first, is it that urgent? If you are expecting an important call, then inform the person at the start of the meeting, so at least it is known that there will be an interruption. (Just be aware of your own perceived self-importance. Every phone call you receive is not urgent.) Sometimes it has been used as a cynical 'exit card' agreed in advance with the PA to cut short the meeting . . . I'm a school leader get me out of this meeting (which is not quite a jungle, but it may have felt you were meeting with a potentially toxic person)!

I would argue that in my era, the lack of telephone use meant every call was more urgent. It was a landline phone in the staffroom or in the office, with no caller ID. Other times it was a handwritten note sent to you by an admin staff (or a student off timetable as the 'office runner') to call the person back. Or that the caller was holding on the line to speak with you and you had to rush to the school office or staff room to take the call (only for it to be cancelled when transferring the call from the school office switchboard. You tried calling them back only to hear the engaged tone. I do recall this frustration many a time when trying to arrange school football fixtures!) In this era of mobile phones, it is easy to even auto-message with a swipe of the screen reply by saying 'Sorry I am busy now, I will call you back'.

Learning outcomes

In every lesson, every activity and in every term of the academic year, children, the students, need to benefit from the teaching input. Otherwise, it is a missed opportunity and risks not achieving the aim that all students will leave the lesson with a gained understanding, but some students did not understand the concept in the lesson. Then it must be delivered again at a later date, when the misunderstanding is evident from an assessment or future dependent curriculum topics that need this prior learning.

Similarly, in every staff development/training session there must be a benefit from the input. Otherwise, this is also a wasted effort as not all staff will finish the training with a gained insight or know-how. Instead, when systems are not fully used or policies not fully applied or worse incorrectly applied, then another refresher course or long e-mail with instructions must be issued.

Learning is or ought to be happening everywhere in schools (and in life in general). Formal learning outcomes that students spend 5+ minutes copying at the start of the lesson and then referring to them later is not the best way for memory development, retention and recollection as research shows.[30] Too often this visible display is meant to provide some reassurance that today's learning has a purpose.

Too often school leaders focus on (exam) outcomes and this is further exasperated by some inspection frameworks which hold the terminal exam results as the proof of strong or weak learning outcomes for the school. This exam hothousing and short-termism may get results, but it reflects badly on the leadership of learning in the school. This culture of 'pass the exams at any cost' is also very toxic. It also puts pressure on parents to pay for additional tutoring (and with the unscrupulous staff tutoring their own students outside of school and even worse with the tacit approval of unethical school leaders). This focus on key results is akin to football clubs who focus on winning the cup rather than finishing higher up in the league and aiming to win the league over a season (progress over time).

As school leaders, reflect on your own learning outcomes too. This is not only in leadership development courses, but also in your work. Make a note literally, electronically, or mentally of any new learning and thinking you have gained from a project implementation or a policy development.

As leaders, reflect on the curriculum and its relevance each year. What needs amending, what needs extending and what needs to be preserved. This also ensures learning outcomes are purposeful and beneficial for staff to plan and deliver and more importantly for students to understand and apply.

Legacy

You may inherit a great legacy and the challenge to maintain it will certainly keep you focused if not provide a few sleepless nights sadly. This could be if you have become a Principal or Headteacher of a school which has been rated 'outstanding,' or if you have become a senior leader, stepping into the role vacated by a previous colleague (who may have moved on due to promotion) of an established successful school. Either way the 'eyes' of the school community are on you. It could be the weight of expectation to maintain the same level of success by either doing it the same way or by doing it differently. A level of honesty and transparency in your authenticity will help you in building your bridge with the school community.

The school leaders who lack that sincerity often have their curriculum vitae as their opening speech to staff and stakeholders, by almost pretending to create a legacy, "in my previous school, I did this . . ". However, it is better to have said that you are looking forward to listening and learning and building on the good practice in this school rather than essentially boast about your track record. Track records are needed in interview to secure your role. They are not needed for you to commence your role!

Meanwhile in your tenure as a school leader, think about what legacy you will leave the school? The mountain concept should be considered here: as the school leader eventually becomes a Headteacher and has moved onto the summit of a higher mountain (i.e. another school or chain of schools or even work for the Government), the legacy of this Head is either a well-trodden path with great succession planning or a route strewn with litter and confusion as to which direction to take.

How many 'outstanding' schools receive a lower inspection rating after the departure of the 'praised' school leader (as per the previous inspection report). This is firm evidence of ineffective succession planning or even worse, being cynical, taking the ball and going home (also known as taking your SLT with you, leaving a void of leadership to be filled).

M

Meeting

School leaders, senior leadership teams (SLT) are the ones in power, paid the most in the school (Note: I did not say SLT are paid a lot!) and need to ensure they meet the wider objectives of the school (improvement plan). SLT are costly meetings. If it were an hourly rate as in some professions such as legal, accountancy or in some jobs such as hourly pay in retail and warehousing, you would reconsider the purpose of the SLT meeting. The most highly paid employees, all gathered around a table to discuss something for a consensus or agreement?

If compared to other sectors, how often does the whole board meet? Of course, a school is not a corporate entity. The needs of a school are very complex. Yet the 2-hour afterschool meeting can 'drag on' with no clear agreement, or in some cases, individuals showing off and in other cases individuals waiting to speak and not listening at all. (Refer to Chapter L.)

What is more damaging and very telling about how effective or not these meetings are is when the outcome is for two of three of the SLT to meet again! To avoid a meeting about a meeting, have a concise agenda of what needs to be discussed, read, thought about and who needs to make the agreement. (Refer to Chapter A.) If you then trim it down, the need for all SLT to be in attendance to discuss all matters is limited.

Also, if there was no agenda provided, then the meeting scheduled in the calendar should be cancelled to avoid a 'weekly gathering' of school leaders. This approach can be taken for any meeting, whether it is with teachers of a particular subject, or form tutors in a year group. If meetings have no agenda, it becomes unstructured and risks whoever speaks first dominating and having their agenda become the team's agenda.

Now consider the meeting itself. The politics of a meeting. Who is to chair, who sits where and next to whom? This is just the seating plan. We have not analysed yet whose agenda items will be discussed. Who will disagree with whom? Or who will be a tunnel and echo what has been said? I said who will be a tunnel and repeat what has been said?! The size of the team also matters as much as who is in attendance. SLT tend to be 'tight' and most move in the same direction with one or two on the fringe of the SLT core team. However, a meeting of MLT (Middle Leadership Team) such as the Subject Leaders, is more challenging for the SLT who chairs such a meeting. This is usually chaired by a Deputy Head).

By its very nature, the MLT is at least double the size of SLT if not triple and all of whom lead teams of their own (often in a very defensive territorial manner despite outwardly professing cross-curricular collaboration). With more people expected to attend, it is more likely many will not arrive on time. Also, the cliques (and internal politics) are more evident, as per who is sat where with more likelihood of whispering conversations whilst others are presenting. Private discussions develop and results in being rude by having their own conversation rather than listening to the main presenter.

To avoid this, ensure all attendees have something to contribute and are not passive attendees or silent witnesses. Another way is to ensure all around the table pay attention is to throw out open questions "what do you think of this?" The usual few will reply, but then you can ask the more reserved team members to share their thoughts. Note this is just like a classroom assessment for learning strategy to ensure all pupils participate.

Also, if you are to chair, ensure unprofessional behaviour is challenged. Perhaps not publicly but privately after the end of the meeting. (Though do avoid the disruptive student staying back at the end of class reprimand as it would be received as more demeaning when talking to colleagues; even if the behaviour was rather childish!)

Membership

Be part of professional bodies. There are quite a few to choose from. Do not choose one for its post-nominal letters or its annual conference either! Choose memberships that benefit you in your role but also the team you lead, which could be a curriculum focus, or a whole school focus. Professional bodies should be supporting the sector and the better ones provides formal avenues for training, development and even tie in with academic or action research.

These bodies not only afford a sense of 'purpose' in connecting schools, teachers and leaders across the region, country or internationally, but they also provide a neutral safe space to seek advice and have peer input in addressing themes that are common to many schools.

Some of these bodies are more than labour unions to help safeguard employee rights and additionally provide a platform for you as professionals to support the profession. In doing so, a collective voice, the opinions of members whether by ballot or by participation, allows further steering of the direction of travel that education is taking.

Other bodies are more established as associations that specialise in pedagogy or specific skills such as literacy, numeracy or critical thinking and support leading practice and research in these focus areas. Others provide a kitemark or 'public badge of membership' which raises the profile of the school and gives a sense of credibility to other stakeholders.

However, they do not always have to be formal (paid) membership. Having collaborative networks across a group of schools in the locality have proven to be highly effective especially for curriculum planning, assessment and inclusion. These can be initiated by a host school and can be rotated within the network of schools who chose to volunteer.

As a school leader, you could initiate a network based on your strength and sharing of good practice or what development needs your school has. For example, if your school is strong on inclusion, you could ensure your school is an inclusion hub for others to visit and learn and share policies and practice. Alternatively, if your school is not so effective in science, you may wish to have a network of science teachers sharing planning, assessment techniques or even the laboratory technicians meeting across schools in mutual support for practical preparation advice.

Mindfulness

Being aware and considerate and not ignorant is also known as having emotional intelligence, often abbreviated to EQ, (emotional quotient). This follows on from IQ, (intelligence quotient, though this is a matter of debate in terms of reliability in what it assesses). When you walk down the corridor do you greet the person you see? Or are you too busy and only greet a person with whom you want to discuss something with?

Another relevant test is the 'face in the crowd' test. This is as much a test of your memory as it is of your mindfulness. How often are you able to recognise someone you know from a school setting outside of school? This could be a parent, a student or in a (large) school a member of support staff if it is not in their usual context. This can be in an aisle in the local supermarket afterschool or a walk in the park during the weekend.

Making a conscientious effort and being considerate will enrich you in many ways as a school leader. You will gain a genuine and sincere 'investment' in the people you are working with, managing and leading. The superficial or selfish approach to people interaction will only get as far as having some tasks completed but will not embed in the culture of the school.

It is not just about being chivalrous as per the knights of old (who went to battle and killed many innocent people), but letting others go in front of you, holding the door open, not pushing in the queue, eating after others have eaten, all resonate well with others in the school community. How often do SLT fill their plate at the buffet lunch in a school training event? Leaders eat last.[31]

Furthermore, as you model this behaviour and consideration, others will follow. I recall saying "hello" to a cleaner and suddenly another SLT member felt obliged to also say hello. Sadly, this was short-lived as she soon recanted back to the brisk walk past the support staff unless she needed something from them. Whilst I made an intentional effort, others imitate but do not necessarily embed the same behaviours to value all staff. My advice from my experience is that learnt habits and behaviours cannot change overnight.

Mindfulness is also evidenced when you contact colleagues out of hours. Is it needed? What does this say about your work organisation? Is it a one-off or a regular need to extend the working day into the evening and weekends? I would always begin with an apology if ever I had to contact a colleague or message or e-mail them out of hours.

N

No

Saying "No" to someone or to a decision is difficult.
It is easier to say yes when asked to do something or give approval when requested by others to please the audience. It is easier to go along with the tide than fight against it.

As school leaders, sometimes you will need to provide a direct answer and decline a request. However, at other times, look for viable alternatives by delaying or deferring a response rather than an 'instant' no. "No, not at this moment," or "no, this is not the priority," are a couple of examples of turning down with some grace and dignity. As much as you learn to deal with disappointment in your role and in your career, it also provides you with this opportunity to help others cope with disappointment of being told "no" (by you).

It also reminds you not to overpromise, but if you encourage something then keep your word to allow others to request and fulfil their demand. (Refer to Chapter U.) Managing expectations is always one of the biggest challenges any school leader will face. Everyone seems to want their priority to be your priority.

Sometimes staff or students (and parents) will say when declined, "well it was allowed last year!" Such an emotive comment even if factually accurate, does not take into consideration the current (or future) circumstances of the school. Context often changes due to budget demands and not being able to afford the 'same' activity as in previous years whether this is a training event, educational visit or a venue hired for a celebration.

Also, priorities may change, where there may be a focus on growing teacher champions in school rather than sending the staff on external courses, certified or otherwise. The cost of cover to enable this whole day out of school versus arranging in-house collaboration are very stark and contrasting.

Being told no by others is even more challenging. When it is the other way around and you are being told "no" or your requests are being declined, (by the Board of Governors, the School Inspectors, a government department, or any other external agency,) this is something which can lead to a tremendous amount of frustration and even anger.

How you cope with this disappointment of being 'turned down' or other significant authority figures disagreeing with you will be as much a demonstration of your tolerance and acceptance of the decision. Alternatively, your resolve and determination to find alternative solutions to having been turned down may prove to be more innovative and creative whilst respecting the decision of the authority.

I recall an example early in my teaching career of being told "no". As a teacher of mathematics, I also volunteered as one of the school football team coaches. One of my teams had reached the semi-final of a cup competition. It was taking place during the school day due to shorter daylight hours in December (in England). I arranged cover for my two afternoon lessons with two colleagues who kindly agreed to cover me as they had non-contact time. I was then told by SLT I could not attend the match as official cover was not available as there was a "Two teachers out of school" cover limit policy and instead a PE support staff member would attend. Of course, my disappointment was immense.

My subsequent staffroom remonstration was as much borne out of frustration as it was from the feeling, I had let down the team by not being able to attend the semi-final, despite hours of afterschool training in Autumn and success in previous rounds. I was also saddened that I had arranged cover, but this was not accepted because of the policy. I was summoned to the SLT's office.

Ironically, I was covered for one of those afternoon lessons to be 'told off' for my remonstration. I also did explain it was ironic that cover was found for me to have this meeting when I could have attended the match, which was met by a rather emotionally unintelligent response, saying "the decision was final".

Navigate

As a school leader, you will embark on many journeys simultaneously. Have a clear plan to help you in your journey ahead and be ready for any diversions if there are roadblocks or barriers.

I use the term 'journey', but this could well be a day, a week, a term, or a project as much as it could mean a year or several years. Just as teachers have a lesson plan for the 'learning journey' in the lesson, as part of a broader medium and long-term plan, you also need to plan for the week ahead, as well as the strategic roadmap for the school.

Sometimes the journey ahead is not as expected, but as a school leader having the skills to navigate will enable your team and/or the organisation to reach the intended destination.

Devise your plan or roadmap for the year ahead highlighting when things happen and annotate your plan during the time of whenever a significant event arises (how long did it take, what challenges arose or even what positives were derived from it).

Yet once you have faced certain obstacles and difficulties, they can become 'regular' occurrences and thus anticipated ones as much as they can be surprises which can attempt to throw you off course and into a (mini) crisis. The expected ones can become like 'speedbumps'. By slowing down, it can help you drive over them.

These could be the objectional staff or parent who wants to challenge with an intent to undermine or a fear of their own i.e. having to change due to a policy update etc. Learning how to engage with your vocal critics is a good way to learn how to navigate. Engage early, anticipate objection and have the grit and determination to see it through, even using an alternative route to the end goal destination.

An example of the navigation is the attainment and progress of the cohort. Each year, you are aware of the final assessment window.

Therefore, how do you navigate the teachers to ensure effective learning and teaching with effective monitoring and assessment? How do you ensure timely intervention and support is provided to maximise achievement? How do you ensure the hidden and non-examined parts of the curriculum are not compromised in the pursuit of qualifications?

The unexpected hurdles are the ones in stormy times, where effective stewardship is needed. Effective school leaders learn how to navigate from past experiences, but also by ensuring they have a Plan A, Plan B and even a Plan C if needed. This is not admission of failure, defeat, or weakness, but learning how to cope.

This can be cascaded to your teams and colleagues who also learn this skill. You can coach them to develop navigation and devise plans in good times and periods of calm and stability; so, when times are more turbulent, they can steer through it.

An unexpected navigation is the COVID-19 pandemic and school closures and switching to online remote/distance learning. The more effective schools were able to arrange this in such a short time turnaround by having made plans which they reviewed and amended on a regular basis as circumstances change i.e. 100% online, blended learning or 100% on site with social distancing. With relevant staff training on technology and video conferencing, it aided better delivery than merely uploading worksheets to be downloaded and completed by the students, for example.

Need

Do you need to? Or do you want to? What I mean by this is, do you really need to attend an event or a meeting? Do you really need to be cc'd in an e-mail? Or is it more from wanting to be involved, or wanting to be seen? Is this a case of FOMO (Fear of Missing Out)? Or on a rather large power trip of self-importance and wanting to be informed or attend the meeting?

I was once told on a training course that by saying you "need to", it is assertive and ensures compliance i.e. when talking to a staff member "I need you to complete this by Friday".

However, I know from personal experience, if I were told that I need to do X, Y and Z, I would probably defer, delay out of choice just because of the blunt demand made with a patronising undertone. (Not everyone would be as obstinate as me!) I only need to be at work, etc. To tell other staff "You need to" can be quite offensive even if no offence is intended.

Leaders tend to want to be involved in many events and activities and certainly like to busy themselves with meetings and are being cc'd in many e-mails. (Refer to Chapter E.) Ask yourself is this healthy, practicable as well as practical? The 'need to know' principle should be applied. It will certainly free up your calendar and e-mail inbox, but also more importantly empower others to fulfil their roles without the SLT overseer!

The other 'need' which will impact your personal life is the 'need to stay back' and then apologise to your family that you "had to stay back". Reflect if this is the reality on the ground, or did you stay back due to a less productive or an inefficient day, causing your work to flow out of hours? "I need to take this phone call" (from a colleague in the evening). Do you really? Can it not wait until the next working day?

Often those in authority with less commitments out of school can easily be absorbed in work tasks and driven to continue with the same intensity out of hours and be less considerate when communicating with peers who do have commitments out of hours. Conversely, the people who are driven and ambitious can become 'workaholics' and neglect their personal life commitments in the process. Either way, it is not a sustainable approach to working.

I was also told once by a leadership coach that I "like to be kept busy". The context was during crisis management of a new start-up school. I was busy, but out of necessity rather than desire. (I can assure all readers!) As a Vice Principal, I was once literally awake for my working day for 23 hours (returning home at 4am only to wake up at 5am for the regular 50-mile (80 km) commute to work the next morning . . . after an hour's sleep! This was not sustainable and there was a very real risk of 'burn out'. Being so worn out due to the lack of rest caused me to be very irritable at work and it showed in some of my decision-making and reactions with other SLT members.

O

Opportunity

Every day brings an opportunity, a fresh start for some or continuation of success for others. Similarly, every setback provides an opportunity for a new solution. Every success provides an opportunity to extend this into other domains. Whenever faced with a challenge, consider it as a problem waiting to be solved, an opportunity to apply critical thinking and innovative skills to support your problem-solving and decision-making.

In another use of the term, school leaders need to ensure opportunity exists for all stakeholders to contribute, to grow and to have success. This is a huge responsibility and hence with an effective SLT, the Senior Leadership Team can have delegated roles and responsibilities to enable this. It is not a one-person show, even though you may feel the weight of the world on your shoulders.

Keeping effective records ensures opportunity for all. Recall back to the classroom. Did you always choose the ones who put their hands up to answer (assuming this was the practice in your class), or did you deliberately choose the 'quiet' inhibited ones or the disruptive ones to keep them focused and on track? How about the others? Neither keen to put their hand up, nor shy or disruptive. The silent majority can often be overlooked.

Cohort analysis in the past twenty-five years has helped target focus on identified groups. Yet have the 'borderline' pass/fail students been assisted whilst those who are significantly below the threshold been ignored? Have the students who have high aptitude been left 'to get on with it' as they will pass anyway'? Ethical questions to reflect upon.

Apply this to staff and the same lessons can be learned. (Excuse the pun!) Are all staff afforded the opportunity to grow and develop? Or is it a 'who shouts loudest gets' in the way baby birds reach out for food from their mother, the quieter ones are neglected, suffer from stunted development and in some tragic cases are forced out of the nest to die.

Who is 'chosen' by SLT to participate in a pilot project, across a cluster of schools, or in conjunction with the local university? Is it based on genuine talent management or picking your 'favourite staff members'? For those who have been in the school for five years or more but have not had these opportunities. Ask why? What can you do as a school leader to provide these opportunities? Or were they provided opportunities but declined? Why? Was it a personal choice, which you can respect, or was it a professional choice? Did they feel they could not 'fit in' with other staff in the project (due to any cliques or being made to feel inferior)?

As a school leader, do level the playing field, ensure all staff are given opportunities to be involved. This could be something as simple as asking a staff member to be 'out of school' to accompany students on an end of term school trip having never been 'chosen' before. Alternatively, it could be asking the staff to participate in a pilot project or enrol on a formal programme of development, having never been 'invited' previously.

Outstanding

One of the most overused words in education is 'outstanding'. Or as I prefer to think, one of the frequent words used incorrectly. If a teacher or a school leader referring to a teacher saying they are "always outstanding" I would question the veracity of such a statement.

Unless all their results are 100% all the time and all their students make progress in all their lessons all the time every day, week, term, or year, then I would agree to the 'always' and would certainly like to meet and learn from that person!

As a school leader, consider how carefully you praise staff in terms of lauding labels of 'outstanding'. This is especially important not to overstate this by overusing the term in correctly when talking to anyone outside of your school including visitors. It can become a false reality and paint an inaccurate picture. It can also damage the perception of your judgement if you have put a member of staff on a pedestal only to be found wanting.

You can certainly be an outstanding teacher, middle or senior leader or an outstanding Principal or Headteacher. You can work in an outstanding department or school and have outstanding results.

In many cases, this judgement is based on the criteria of an inspection framework (or a staff appraisal/performance management policy for lesson observations). Therefore, if most or all the criteria are met, you are awarded 'outstanding'.

Consider 'outstanding' in a different aspect. Outstanding is a synonym of stand out. How do you stand out? How do you make sure your actions and impact stand out? Do you follow a tried and tested methodology handed down to you or lifted from a training course? Or do you ensure that you and your staff make sure the school stands out for the students and the community?

We are all unique from our own appearance, DNA and neurology. Your challenge, as a leader, is to find that USP (unique selling point) as is stated on MBA courses, that makes you stand out as a leader.

The chances are that you have been in the shadow of significant others as you strived towards leadership. You may even be a professional 'clone' or imitate a mentor or role model as you become a leader. Furthermore, some training courses that you have attended may have provided templates and expected methodologies which you may tweak but adopt almost in totality. Consequently, this leads to having a predictable modus operandi.

Now this is not a bad thing per se. However, your unique abilities are what will make you stand out and strive to become a great leader and not just a trained leader or technocrat.

I was asked in an interview for a Deputy Head position, "Are you an outstanding teacher?" I replied "No . . . I am not consistently outstanding. I have had some outstanding lessons, but most of my lessons are good or very good. However, I can say that I have a consistently outstanding attitude with determination for the success of all students".

I was successful in securing the role, despite the long pause after replying "No" and the shock on the chair of Governors face when I said no, but the pause allowed me thinking time to explain why I was not going to boast a false claim of "always being outstanding" (which would imply it was the norm and not the exception).

As I stepped into senior leadership, I have felt the tension to be 'consistently outstanding' in lessons when committing to whole school responsibilities. With a partial teaching load in multiple classrooms (and even teaching mathematics in a science laboratory) and often with shared classes, the risk of diminished teaching quality is real. (These are not excuses, but rather explaining the context of a typical SLT timetable.)

Furthermore, having a meeting or office at the other end of the school site, often meant that sadly, I was late to lessons and I began my lesson with an apology for arriving late! I did, however, always make up for this professional shame by having revision classes after school, in the evening, in the school holidays and at weekends to make sure all my students (and others whom I did not teach) had the maximum opportunity to be successful in their examinations.

Outliers

We all remember a great teacher who inspired us when we were young ... even a 'favourite' teacher. We also recall (with horror, or now as an adult with a sense of relief), the teachers who were incompetent or angry. These two ends of a teaching body define the brilliant and awful examples you find elsewhere in the profession (as well as other sectors). The same can be applied by substituting the word 'teacher' with the word 'Principal' or 'leader'.

Not only as defined in the book by Malcolm Gladwell[32] (and it is a good read) but in your cohort of students, staff and parents, seek out those at the very edge of the population or those that seem to buck the trend.

Your own leadership ability can be evaluated with competency frameworks, psychometric and cognitive ability tests and measures to evaluate your emotional quotient. From this, you too can see where you fit on the 'scale'. It is a useful self-development tool as well.

The gifted and talented student or staff will always be able to thrive based on their own innate ability. With the challenge and encouragement, they can achieve truly exceptional, pioneering and world-class standards.

At the 'other end of the (academic) scale' there are many students who are diagnosed as having Special Educational Needs (SEN) but will thrive if given the opportunity in the appropriate climate for learning. Many a 'college dropout' who failed academically went on to have remarkably successful careers.

Also, as mentioned earlier in this chapter, it is also especially important to provide an opportunity for the majority of the population in the middle (assuming a normal distribution curve) who are often overlooked.

However, seek out those outliers to raise the bar further for collective success. Individual intelligent staff can shape and lead a culture of 'can do' and 'want to do'. They can think and 'join the dots' in ways that can be 'from the ground up' so long as school leaders facilitate such a culture. They can also lead on initiatives such as 'innovation', a term more used in schools in the past decade than ever before (coinciding with the change of technology and the advancement of mobile devices and the internet).

Such clever colleagues should not be mocked for having an interest or habit in something less mainstream than the usual staff room discussions on popular culture. Such staff should not also be belittled for being first to complete a CPD course that all staff are expected to have done in a specified timeframe.

The same applies to students who are consistent high performers. The challenge needs to be there. The common mistake is to give the student more content, "complete the next chapter". However, by developing other skills such as being a co-teacher, you are enabling them to share their understanding with peers. This is a deeper level of learning than whizzing through a textbook and answering dozens of questions.

It is cool to be clever. (That is genuine intelligence as opposed to thinking you are clever.) Excellence in the pursuit of knowledge, understanding, further studying and obtaining certifications and qualifications should be encouraged and recognised. Talented students and staff in arts, sports, linguistics and other expressive and performing settings should also be praised too.

P

People

Some professions have limited interaction with people or at best with their same team only around their same desk or station. Schools are living institutions, full of life, growing and nurturing people. This really sets us apart from other sectors. I recall a comparison made between doctors and teachers which is quite apt: "Doctors make people become better. Teachers make better people". Though I would modify this to read as: 'Doctors help people become better. Teachers nurture better people'.

As a school leader, if you do not know the name of your cleaners then there is a disconnect and void that must be filled. Be able to know at least 3 facts about every staff member. This can be achieved by meeting every staff member for 15 minutes in your first term. (Refer to Chapter E.) Investing time and effort in people more than money will enable you to be a more effective leader.

As often repeated throughout this book, to apply policy and procedure will enable you to manage, but not gain that true followship that leaders have. I say this, in terms of leading people rather than having followers on social media. The often-misconstrued notion of followship which is more about popularity online rather than leading people!

Every person brings value to the school. The personal lives and the professional 'stakeholder' are interwoven as they ought to be. The student in school is a son or daughter out of school, the teacher in school is the wife or husband, brother or sister, mother, or father out of school. To assume these can be kept permanently separate is a fallacy. Of course, the purpose of school is for learning and teaching amongst many other developmental experiences. By remaining professional and true to the purpose, children learning (as students) and adults teaching (as teachers), we can remain 'on message,' focused but the personal life will affect the professional life and impact the workplace.

Great schools rightfully look at the context of a student outside of school, family dynamics and what support can be offered by the school. Great leaders would apply the same care and compassion for staff. We cannot assume to be professional without being human first. We are not robots!

Your interaction, your communication and your management of people whether this is peers, parents, or pupils, in fact your every action in school is noted by others not only by those you directly meet but indirectly from word of mouth, letters and social media too.

Applying policy and process will help in your management of people but it will be your personality that will enable you to demonstrate leadership. An example of the distinction between management and leadership: Management is when you decide, whereas leadership is how you decide.

Also, for any such judgements which will affect many people, do have some evidence or wisdom behind it rather than it seems to be an opinion or somewhat anecdotal. You are always being judged, but in your authority, you can be judge and jury. Choose well. Consult with others before deciding something that will impact so many people.

Presentations

Too much text? Too much talk? Too much detail? Does the content cause eye strain? Is the sound of the presenter's voice affecting the ability of the audience to focus and comprehend?

We have all attended poor presentations, but consider if the presenter, was you?! As school leader you will present (formally) often. In fact, you may have had to present in interview to have obtained your current leadership position in the first place.

Less is best. Presenting should leave staff with a sense of wonder and inspiration rather than a barrage of questions such as how, what and when or even worse why? This means that some of the audience may not have understood the key message at all!

People, Presentations, Pressure

In my days, it was the flip chart and/or overhead projector with the occasional treat of a coloured acetate. Now it is rare to see the PC plugged into a projector, but rather it is wirelessly presenting from your laptop or tablet device, things have progressed far in terms of technology hardware!

With regards to software, the overuse of animation, zooming in or out, often leaves some with nausea. Text 'flying' in from all angles of the screen and templates with different fonts and colours can leave the audience with a sense of confusion and a disjointed presentation.

Before you consider the delivery, first consider the purpose of the presentation. What message are you hoping to deliver? What do you want the audience to have understood by the end of your presentation?

The 'whole school' or 'all staff' meetings (usually at the start or end of term), are the most expensive meetings in the school. With at least 80% of the staff body in attendance, that hour must be highly effective and purposeful. There are usually key messages from school leaders, make it meaningful and relevant.

Avoid an information overload. This can either be an exceedingly long individual presentation or a series of concurrent presentations by a group of people. Often the latter happens when there are competing SLT members trying to get their agenda across to the masses. It can be crude self-promotion and liking the sound of their own voice or it can appear like a queue waiting for their turn to present one after another. Either way the first presentation may have got the most attention, but by the end, even that initial message could have been lost.

The delivery is very much dependent on the person presenting and their contents to present. Some may need to rehearse the presentation. If this is needed, then find trusted peers to practise it to. Formality versus joviality is as much about you as a person as it is the setting you are in. You may be more 'serious' with Governors than perhaps you would be with staff.

Assuming you have clarity in communication, if the content is dire, then the message intended to be delivered will fall flat. How much needs to be 'presented' and how much detail can be found in a document which can be shared afterwards?

Some advice on formats includes the 6x6 (6 words per bullet point and 6 bullet points per slide). Others say to spend no more than 1 minute per slide, which following this rule would be about 10 seconds per bullet point. This could be quite rapid and may lose the audience. If unsure, rehearse again and again. Now with the audio voiceover option, you can literally play it back to yourself.

Lastly, the style of the presentation, is it didactic with the usual Q&A (Questions and Answers) at the end? Is it didactic but encourages the audience to ask any questions as you go along? This can result in a risk of continuous interruption or going off track with the interjections, but it becomes more democratic for the audience. Or is it deliberately interactive where you pose questions to the audience?

Great leaders can present without the need to have a supporting software presentation document. They are like the orators of the olden days, able to capture the attention of the audience. Others can present with a few images and literally a few words per slide only and capture the imagination of the audience with an image or short video presented. You can aspire to this if you have not already mastered such an art.

Pressure

As a school leader you face a lot of pressure. Yet the most intense pressure is to shoulder the pressure and stress from your teams. There is nothing worse than showing your anger and frustration with others in person or with the sending of infamous cc e-mails.

Hold back. Whilst sometimes it is exceedingly difficult to hold back from reacting or responding. This resolve has been further developed in recent times. The COVID-19 pandemic has taught us all to be more resilient and find inner strength.

Being a school leader and doing the job 'properly,' is a great burden and takes its toll over the years. Caring for others, often putting yourself second most of the time in the service of others is commendable. Applying the seven Nolan principles of public office[33] (Selflessness, Integrity, Objectivity, Accountability, Openness, Honesty, Leadership) are ones not only school leaders, but I would argue leaders in all sectors (including private) should adhere to.

It is quite easy to understand why the pressure, the expectation is so immense given the huge responsibility, but to reassure you as a school leader, there is a lot of respect and admiration from those outside of education (even if that angry parent, or uncooperative staff may make you feel otherwise)!

We all have our own coping mechanisms and it would be naïve of me to suggest you all take up a sport to relieve the stress, for example. Though it is important to keep fit as mentioned previously. (Refer to Chapter F.) Instead, take a moment on how you cope with stress. Is it by way of food and beverage? Being active? Escaping into a book, movie or 'binging' on a TV series being streamed? Whatever works for you in your personal life, so long as it does not harm (and of course is not illegal) then use this to relieve stress.

However, personal life tension resulting from professional life stress is worth reflecting on. The risk of being so serious in the working day, having your 'game face' (playing the role of the teacher, the school leader, which is ironic, as games involve fun), could result in erratic behaviour outside of school in your personal lives.

I have many friends who are doctors and the stories they have shared (without sharing patient details of course!) about teachers and the almost double lives they lead in 'letting loose' at the weekends or more usually in the school holidays is quite disturbing. The almost perverse risky behaviours clearly illustrate the inability to manage their tension in the workplace and having the urge to 'go wild' outside of term time as a coping mechanism.

This also applies in other sectors (both public and private) as well. How many 'professionals' are 'caught' doing something inappropriate in their personal lives as their professional life is filled with a sense of tension and over-seriousness and they lack that sense of warmth, humour and relaxation needed in the working day.

Q

Quality Assurance

Quality assurance (QA) is vital to ensure standards are met. These are the standards of the school, your own professional standards and in the pursuit of excellence against national or global standards.

The WWW EBI approach can be a tad insincere (*What went well. Even better if*), as it assumes the person doing the QA has the solutions to make it 'better' than the current practice. I may have some ideas in some areas, but I would seldom say "Even Better If" unless I have some actual insight that it is better and I have used it to some level of success previously. A line manager and mentor of mine once said to me to use WWW HYTA (*What want well. Have you thought about?*) which I have since refined to WWW HYC (*What Went Well. Have you considered?*)

In your new role and especially if in a new setting, you have a great opportunity to quality assure everything and anything around you. This could be within your immediate roles and responsibilities or looking at specific processes, operational, academic, or even financial.

The obvious question could be "why is this being done this way?" The reply would so easily be "because it always has been!" That is not meant to say that the respondent is being sarcastic, but rather if you do what you have always done, you will get what you have always got. If people do not know of any better, alternative, modern or efficient ways, they will continue in the same way they have done. Recall back to your teaching, where students make a common mistake or inefficient approach leading to running out of time, your role as a teacher is to facilitate improvement. The same applies to you as a leader.

As the world is dynamic and ongoing, to assume you have the 'perfect' school model will be limiting in the long term if not the medium term. Other schools who constantly reflect and diagnose will improve and go beyond the expected standards of outstanding. Now the pioneering schools are using words such as "world class". Though I have also seen schools that do not fit that criteria also claiming (falsely) that they too are 'providing a world class education'. Yet it amounts to qualifications and a few extracurricular projects. Many factors would affect what is incredibly high quality and pioneering to enable world class status. Consider the alumni of a school and this is a good indication as to which universities and careers they enter (though discrimination and other barriers do exist even for highly qualified alumni which could limit their progress unfortunately since leaving school successfully).

If you are established in your school, it may be difficult to have that objective view to ask questions (even if stating the obvious) about. Consider having an external view to provide a 'fresh eyes' approach. This does not have to be paid consultants, but if budgets allow have a reputable school improvement partner or an experienced retired school leader to come in and gauge the current climate.

Often budgets are (mis)spent on nepotism and cronyism with friends being asked to come in and provide training, consultancy and professional development. The obvious risk here aside from any ethical considerations, is the lack of objectivity if they are 'friends' in the feedback provided. How often are friends critical or are they rather biased in their support of one another? (I would expect a true friend to provide honest feedback and tell me how it really is even if it is rather uncomfortable. I may not share this information publicly or with others, but I would use it as reflection to modify any future intentions and actions.)

One (free) approach is to have NPQH trainee headteacher placements attend your school. Even if it is 9 days officially, it allows an 'outside' view of the school.

Another way is school intervisitations. A school intervisitation allows you to benchmark, but also to evaluate your school context, in different ways perhaps to your first 100 days. Ask peers to come in and critique or offer insight to your school context. By you reciprocating the visit to other schools and seeing things from a 'fresh eyes' aspect, it allows you to also ask the same questions that your peers may have asked when they visited your school.

Also, if you have other inspirational observations or queries that you have picked up when visiting schools, bring the same 'queries' back to your school and ask the same questions and see what solutions are needed.

Within school, QA should be encouraged across the curriculum and across the houses or year groups too. Having Middle Leaders offer their view of holding a similar position but in another subject or year group, provides that culture of openness and builds trust amongst peers. For example, this could be two different subject leaders or even two different year leaders who quality assure processes, data, outcomes and evaluate staff in those teams. Similarly, across the whole school, QA by theme is something not so often considered by school leaders, but it could be provide a unique cross-section of schoolwide QA.

QA of teaching and or data are the obvious ones that all schools do and they tend to be formally provisioned in the school calendar, but how about by themes? QA of the wellbeing of students and staff on a random day and follow up a month later. QA of the use of technology across the curriculum. QA of the sustainability of the school and commitments to environmental friendliness. QA of the start of the school day or the end of the school day. Other powerful ways to have effective QA is to have all SLT to shadow a student all day or shadow a staff member all day.

There are so many facets within a complex organisation such as a school which need QA on a regular basis. It should happen at least once a year but aim to have it once a term and even every half-term would be the aspiration. QA can be light touch from a collection of observations, through to a detailed improvement plan. It should result in at least some purposeful reflection and discussion and consideration to amend policy or practice in the future. The discussion should be with both the SLT but also a 'working committee' of a range of staff who have some relevance to the QA topic.

Lastly, the QA by students and parents, will always provide a very raw view of matters with no professional restraint! Engage them formally also by way of QA by surveys, roundtable meetings and feedback requests.

Question

QA and any aspect of your work must enable questions. By having a culture of trust, openness underpinned with reflection and a willingness to gain a deeper understanding, a school community will thrive. (The opposite is true, which will result in suspicion and diminished opportunities of growth and improvement.)

At least one of the following six key components, which I was taught as the 'Articles of Learning,' can be found in all questions:

- Who?
- What?
- Where?
- When?
- How?
- Why?

By having this culture to gain a deeper understanding, questions should be encouraged from students in every lesson, in every subject and for all staff to also reflect and gain a deeper insight into their work. The fundamentals for the articles of learning and gain further knowledge and have a genuine inquiry-based learning.

What should you, as school leaders, question?
- The narrative: Is what is being presented or told to you valid?
- The policy: Is what is being prescribed relevant or purposeful?
- The context: Is the current status enhancing or limiting success?

Who is presenting the narrative or leading the policy? What do schools need to do (if an external government policy)? What do staff need to do (if you are leading on an internal policy)? Where and when are things needed? Is it all teachers, a certain key stage and is it by the end of term or planning ahead for next year?

How are we going to achieve this? The most common approach that many school leaders take is they jump to the how? Being solution-focused and driven for success in resolving matters, sometimes they can proceed without asking the key question. Why?

Start with Why?[34] We can assume it is a policy that has to be adhered to and implemented. However, why is it needed? Does it benefit your school community? I am not encouraging non-conformism, rebellion, or dissent. Far from it, by having some answers for the Why? You have a stronger foundation with which to proceed rather than an illiterate compliance.

But also encourage others to question you, as well as things around you. School leadership should not be a defensive overture to tough questions.

As leaders, you have authority and it is expected you ask questions. Yet be expected to have others ask you questions or question the approach. It does not mean you have to give an immediate response or more usually react by giving a response that you may regret later.

Qualifications

'Lifelong learning' is also used a lot in schools, on their websites and by school leaders. Yet how is it practised? It could be used in specific cases, where someone was not successful in their formal schooling but then goes on to graduate from university twenty years later. Such a story is worthy to be acknowledged and celebrated. Such turnaround stories can also be found in individuals who led a life of crime or addiction but now play contribute positively to society. These stories need celebrating as they inspire a message that it is never too late!

Qualifications and certifications are formal ways to recognise learning and achievement. School leaders need to enable a culture for continuous learning and formal certification to ensure a school community thrives. The 'qualified' teacher assumes a finite position.

This is rather fanciful as the teacher qualified in a certain time and place with a particular curriculum training. Curricula change, qualifications are discontinued, or new ones introduced and on top of this the role of the internet and technology have been two of the largest disruptions in education and society exceeding any previous industrial revolution.

Schools, as they stand, are the first formal channel of initial qualifications and certifications that a teenager has to experience. Students may not meet their expectations and the sense of disappointment can be severe. As a school leader, you can develop the architecture to provide the appropriate support mechanisms for any failure to be coped with and the opportunity to rectify this is by re-sitting the examination or pursuing other learning pathways.

Whilst indeed we only have one lifetime from childhood to adulthood; the fresh start that each lesson, each day, each week and each term brings sends a message of hope, forgiveness and the opportunity to atone, to use a religious term. It also provides a much-needed fallibility that we have shortcomings, make mistakes and have gaps in understanding. The intent and ability to seek further learning is what is key and the mindset and character learners need, whether these are students, parents, or staff.

I recall some examples of school leaders in keynote speeches celebrating their failures. Whilst it is healthy to (publicly) acknowledge less successful moments in your life, it sends a risky message to students and staff you are leading that you are proud of failing in an almost boastful way.

Do not celebrate failure but rather learn from it and re-take to get the qualification you need. "I failed exams in X subjects". Rather "I wasn't successful first time around but resat and achieved success later". This is a good role model of a lifelong learner determined to obtain a good set of qualifications.

The example I recall as a teacher was as soon as the GCSE exams were sat by the students and couriered away, we all had a go at the paper in our department (in exam conditions). Not only was it about who could finish the paper first but of course who could score 100%. This was friendly competition and a healthy vibe amongst colleagues, which further validated why the department I had the privilege to be part of was indeed rated 'outstanding'.

In a similar way, you will see staff, especially some senior leaders and experienced staff, who appear too busy, too (self) important, to spare the time for a (collective) online professional development session which may culminate in an online assessment. Examples being a technology certification, or a child protection refresher course. The excuse given "I will finish the module later on as I have a few things to attend to now". Though this is more likely to be a combination of a fear of failure and snobbery.

Such staff feel such things are beneath them to be in a collective training space, whether it is a workshop or an online course in an IT lab. As a school leader, you must not allow pride to get in the way as in "why should I have to take this assessment? (I am already qualified.)"

Lead by example in lifelong learning. Further academic qualifications (Masters, Doctorate studies), further professional qualifications (the suite of NPQs) or the newer certifications from various blended learning modules and those in the digital tech era too. I intentionally learned skills on how to use technology to enhance teaching and learning despite perhaps not needing to use them in my day-to-day work as I was not a main scale teacher.

However, by making a point of learning these skills and obtaining certification, it provided a further level of credibility with staff that these were not the domain of the Head of ICT only, but as school leaders we ought to undertake these. By doing so we have the same fear of failure, but also the joy of being successful and receiving a certification. I went on to share the experiences to the wider community by publishing an article.[35]

The future of learning will become increasingly based on online microcredentials, mini courses online with some 'homework' and MCQs (multiple-choice questions) with certificates of completion, but some leading to actual qualifications too. As a school leader, seek these out and aim to have a new certification from such micro-credential courses every year or 18 months.

Share your learning and achievement with others and have a culture of all staff seeking to gain new skills and knowledge. This provides a truly continuous development and growth of the workforce. It also ensures that everyone is afforded a chance to obtain further certifications.

R

Routines

As a new school leader, you will have developed routines, customs and habits throughout your career, which have served you well to date. In many leadership development courses, school leaders are 'trained' to be risk averse. Furthermore, in your context, you will be keen to ensure structures are established, expectations made clear and any protocols are adhered to consistently. Some researchers even refer to rituals[36] that elite professional athletes adopt to develop, maintain and retain high performance.

Routines are effective in helping provide a sense of normality, expected behaviours and therefore some predictability in outcomes. The challenge is which of your routines are deeply personal to you in your role or capacity? And which are the ones that the school as an organisation will need to adopt? Some will only apply to you, but some routines will benefit the wider school community.

As teachers in the classroom, you were very adept in establishing routines for the students in the class. In Primary, it certainly begins with more emotional and physical boundaries and having clear and consistent expectations and in Secondary the behaviour for learning, the responsibility for students for their own learning and the 'norms' in a classroom/learning environment.

When managing adults, expectations also need to be set. The obvious way is to tell team members what is required. However, a more collegiate approach of agreeing 'ground rules' does tend to have 'buy in' and more collective ownership.

For example, in many courses I have attended, confidentiality and no mobile phone use standout as key expectations throughout the duration of the course sessions (but the latter falls by the wayside unless the course facilitator reminds people).

Great classes have great learning underpinned by established routines in most cases. Great schools have great outcomes also underpinned with established routines. These are not only the behaviour norms, but clear expectations that the whole (class) community understand. Such that if a new member joins the class, it is 'expected' how they will learn.

As a school leader your routines help shape the culture of the school, but it is a dynamic equilibrium between routines ↔ culture. The culture of the school can affect your work routines as much as your routines will affect the culture of the school. (Refer to Chapter S: Spheres of influence.)

An example is what you expect others to conform to can be enacted with policy as much as a verbal/e-mail directive. Routines should not stifle creativity and innovation. Ironically, routines display expected behaviours, but this can be an open-ended outcome. Is there a freedom to research, innovate and take risks?

These can also be part of the pedagogy routines, for example. So, the expected norm is to take risks, the outcomes can be very imaginative and even unpredictable. Clearly context is key, you would take less of a risk with end of term examination preparation than with a mid-term topic. However, maybe this also provides an opportunity to prepare and deliver revision lessons in an innovative way.

Beyond the classroom, in meetings you lead or attend, you can observe the routines and consider what needs changing. These tend to be more emotive as staff feel a sense of belonging in these meetings, with a culture that they have shaped.

Research
Every year we learn more and more about the world around us and the school amongst us. Data analysis has become a data science. Great school leaders are always looking to see what is 'out there' and what they can apply in their context. Some are fortunate to be true pioneers and lead on research and be at the forefront of new discoveries, or validations of their existing practice, which then moves on from good

practice to evidence-based best practice.

Carry out research in your school setting every year. This does not have to be by you, but it ought to be encouraged and/or facilitated by you. This research can be action research[37] in the classroom by a teacher or a group of teachers within a subject. It provides authentic and purposeful research and the 'buy in' from peers should be more positive as it is in their school, in their classes with their students. It is also a strong indicator of the culture of the teaching and if it is truly reflective and teachers make efforts to further enhance their practice.

School leaders should research their context across the school and amongst schools to further develop good and best practice. This should accompany the school's self-evaluation cycle. The key is to ensure the focus of the research is clear. Start by considering a valid question to ask. (Refer to Chapter Q: Question.) It could be researching outcomes on a 3-year basis and what was done differently, how and why? What remained the same i.e. who delivered the classes, when was revision factored in? What other factors affected each cohort? What was the context of each cohort?

The purpose of research can also be for external purposes to further academic studies at a university. It can be to gather evidence to evaluate government policy. Put your school forward to participate in such initiatives. Not only does it raise the profile of your school, but it also allows your school to have another external agency bring their experts to offer some valuable, unbiased insight into your practice.

Research also has a few intertwined works, also commencing with R, which can fall into this domain: review, re-evaluate, reconsider, relevance and reading (around the subject or reading about such leading areas that will affect all schools such as artificial intelligence/big data and neuroscience).

Along with any research is the data; collection, validation and analysis, which form part of the evidence to validate your initial question. It could be qualitative such as survey feedback, or the more commonly found quantitative numerical values which are often used in displaying percentages for example. To make the qualitative data survey more valid, ask a how and why rather that a what?

For example, instead of:
- What did you like about today's training on using devices in lessons?
- Rather reframe it to: How would you intend to use devices in lessons?
    - If you do not intend to use devices, how would you enable dynamic and interactive learning in lessons?

Then ask the 'why' to initiate a deeper reflection and response:
- Why do you feel technology has or has not enhanced learning?

As a new school leader, spend the first 100 days (and beyond) by listening, observing and taking notes. This may be anecdotal evidence at times, but you can always research the data afterwards. For example, you may have seen some inadequate learning in a class or a subject, you can then go back and check their attainment and progress data to see if it was a 'bad day at the office' or is there also a trend of poor outcomes? If so, is a more formal review needed to ascertain what support can be provided for the teachers? The eagerness to make the change and have an impact can lead to having to 'change the change' (a few weeks later) as it was not as well considered (without data or evidence to support the initial change).

The review of the current practice, policies and systems as well as staffing will support any argument for change or an amendment to current practice. (Refer to Chapter C.)

I know I have often gathered thoughts on things that are inspirational or the opposite and sadly caught my attention as I thought it was woeful, or a health and safety (H&S) hazard. I often typed a few notes on my device or on the reverse side of some scrap paper. (I keep and reuse until no more scope to be used before recycling!)

My photos of school issues have varied from a great display in the corridor, or a thoughtful poster with a memorable quote or some great evidence of learning through to clutter in a classroom, damaged furniture, or any other H&S hazards. Usually with the advancement of messenger apps, it can be forwarded to the relevant staff to take action and address the issue with some level of discretion and dignity. Conversely, a formal e-mail to the staff concerned with a positive feedback praising what I saw in their class/corridor with the attached photo.

Referee

Not another football analogy, but as a senior school leader, you will be asked to provide a reference for current and former employees. If you are a Principal or Headteacher you would be the first reference and as a member of SLT the second reference but possibly the first depending on the role applied for.

The job hunt is manic, every Term 2, it is in its earnest to fit in with notice periods in the summer term for new staff to join after the summer holiday. The push and pull factors for staff movement are many, but they usually focus on salary, responsibility, school reputation and more recently location. Do not be bitter or begrudge others who move on.

Of course, as a leader it is about talent management and offer incentives to have effective staff remain in your organisation. Sometimes being innovative and creative, you can provide a niche position or role to retain that staff member. Sometimes it is not always salary increments, nor time i.e. a lower teaching load, (but of course both help!) rather the role to lead or develop or oversee a project can be just as appealing.

Insecure leaders play the guilt trip "after all that we have done for you". It is not about this, but rather think of it as a transactional process. Any investment in staff development has had positive gains and effects on other staff and most importantly students in your school. If they want to move on, remember that they take the values and principles learned under your leadership, which is something to be cherished. The excellence you espouse may be further spread as you have grown leaders to go into other schools.

Similarly, be honest as the cynical need to "move someone on" by giving an exaggerated reference would only damage your own professional reputation but also any incompetent staff "is someone else's problem" and they could risk causing damage to children's life opportunities elsewhere. If it is a case of encouraging someone to leave the school, you can always write what you can about the person by not saying something. This factual statement of what were their positives even if they are a few is better than adding any false or negative reports. Yet you owe it to that person to try and develop them into competent practitioners whether they stay with your school or move on.

There is the rare, but rather difficult, discussion with such staff that teaching or working in schools may not be their forte rather than enabling them to have them the false belief that they can teach somewhere else having perhaps reached their optimum performance in the classroom or sadly rarely delivered good consistent lessons. Of course, if it is safeguarding related, criminality or any termination of staff for gross misconduct or malpractice then this is the obvious reference as such individuals should not be working in schools or with children.

The worst thing you can do as a school leader is not respond to a reference request (out of envy, hatred or selfishly not seeing it as a priority). The second worse thing is to reply with a dishonest reference.

S

Solution

In your role as a leader, the range of solutions you may need to consider will range from an emergency or crisis management; safeguarding and health and safety; human resources; financial; behaviour (students, or parents or even staff!) and liaising with external authorities. The list is long. The issues are often complex requiring an immediate response as well as a more permanent solution. Consult others, discuss possible ('what if') scenarios and solutions.

Problem solving and troubleshooting is part of leadership. Original thought is difficult to generate but thinking how to apply existing thought to your context helps develop the element of uniqueness that is needed to find a bespoke solution.

Bespoke does imply that you need to disregard a generic 'off the shelf' approach. Sometimes you can tweak existing practice to fit a generic solution. This will provide short-term and even medium-term success but adopting a system and then adapting it for your context will always provide the more embedded solution. (Refer to Chapter T.)

As a new leader, you have the perfect opportunity to be a troubleshooter, (not a troublemaker, though tech disrupters would argue on the contrary!) as you will be asking why this is happening or more importantly, why is this not happening?! The weakest response is "because we have always done this" which must not be accepted.

As a leader and someone in authority, it comes with the territory of being the one to go-to person to fix matters or resolve issues which may not be systemic, but person related. Skills of diplomacy, tact and consideration go a long way to find solutions amicable and acceptable to all or the majority so long as it is in the best interest of the school.

As a new school leader, impact is something you are keen to achieve as you establish yourself in the school. However, solutions that are imposed do not get the 'buy in' for the long term and consideration ought to be given to whether that solution is worth the fallout.

Other advice I was given was to focus on what many would think are less important or lower priority items i.e. 'sweat the small stuff' and the larger issues will take care of themselves. An example is student behaviour or discipline as some (still) call it. Wearing the correct footwear and zero tolerance on punctuality sends a message that if students cannot 'get away' with this, then they will conform to the wider issues. This is of course a simplistic approach.

It could also be argued that this level of assertive authority will lead to teenagers in 'rebelling' and even rejecting rather than reflecting and conforming. (I recommend engaging with student voice/leadership on matters of dress code/appearance to have that 'buy in' that it is derived from their peers rather than adults imposing on the students and often with out of touch 'in my day' approach to school uniform matters.)

I would rather define that as a school leader, consider having solutions focused even on the smaller, lower priorities. The solutions may not be needed now, but nonetheless the fact you have solutions is something that you can draw upon.

Spheres of influence

Affect those whom you can rather than those whom you cannot. As a new school leader, you should want to know the whole school community. Unless you are a Headteacher or Principal, your 100% coverage of the school will not necessarily be as you want. Even as a Headteacher, your influence with the Board of Governors or with external authorities may not be how you want either.

Leaders are always told (or trained) to focus on the 'big picture'. Invariably this can mean to seek solutions where solutions are not necessarily in your immediate control.

Consider concentric circles, with you in the middle (or think of an archery target board, with you as the bullseye, which may be more apt).

Then your immediate circle is the SLT and work outwards on who you can influence to ensure specific actions are taken, policies are implemented, or protocols are met. This is a good example of working through others to achieve an objective.

Also, as much as you may feel otherwise, sometimes staff or any stakeholder may want to hear it from another person! Listening to you or reading e-mails from you can fade into the background for some. Your 'rank' may draw on many to pay attention momentarily, but the impact or effect could be lost. Sometimes the direct line manager or peer is better than being told from 'high above' in SLT or by the Principal. It is the same message but delivered by another person who they seem to be more receptive to. It is easy to see this as undermining or become paranoid at an apparent disrespect towards you, but there is no harm in enabling others. Ask other staff members to discuss or meet with another colleague to say what you wanted to or have done (first time) but to limited effect.

This is a good example of an effective approach to 'work through others'.

Now consider another approach to influence by using the Venn diagram. Imagine you are one circle with a colleague/another stakeholder as the other circle. The overlapped area of both circles (known as the 'intersection' in mathematics language), is the shared responsibilities, priorities or the 'middle ground'. If there is a large overlap, this means there is a lot in the middle ground, between you and the other stakeholder. Therefore, you ought to have a lot of influence when interacting with this stakeholder.

The more effective leaders learn the skill to indirectly affect. By which I mean that in overlapping roles of others, your actions can lead to others not having to act, but conversely, if you facilitate the action or provide the environment for the other stakeholder to take action, it means you do not need to and the objectives in the intersection are met.

In this same model, you can quantify 'shared' areas and what are sole responsibilities or remits of each stakeholder. If there are a lot of shared items, i.e. 'quality teaching', 'excellent learning', 'technology', in the overlapped areas, then effective delegation can be offered but also your influence will be strong. If for example, the only shared remit is 'assemblies', then clearly you and your colleagues are working in isolation or a less collaborative way within your own remits.

If there is less in the common ground, consider how more actions can happen in a collaborative way. In this model, consider how by the end of the first term, more 'items' are placed in the intersection. This Venn Diagram approach can be used for any two inter-connected entities such as SLT and Teachers.

Now consider a three-way Venn diagram with Staff, Students and Parents as the respective 'circles'. This could be useful for developing or reviewing a policy directory and then place policies in the diagram. Of course, all school policies indirectly are the domain of all stakeholders, but you can ask the following questions:

Which policies are exclusively for one stakeholder?
- Staff appraisal or performance management = Staff.

Which are for two stakeholders?
- Student absence = Parents and Students.
- Teaching and learning = Staff and Students.
- Admissions = Staff and Parents.

Which are for all three?
- Safeguarding, Special Educational Needs, Health & Safety

This approach also helps organise your current thoughts and where you hope to be with a plan, a before and after Venn diagram.

What is certain is that your sphere of influence will grow in the school over time. Always use this in the service of the school community rather than for self-gain or an 'easy ride' by delegating to others all the time.

School

Whilst financial viability is important and modern school leaders need good business acumen, do not forget you are in a school! Young children commencing Primary education and completing Secondary education as young adults - an amazing life journey if ever there was one!

The need to have an MBA or the even more sinister role of 'corporate leadership' models where non-teachers are leading schools or groups of schools is something that cannot distract you from your purpose of leading a school.

The non-specialist leading a school from 'outside the profession' could be considered on a par with a non-healthcare professional managing a hospital, or an unqualified football coach managing a team or even worse . . . a non-teacher leading the education department. (Since the end of World War Two, only four out of thirty-five Education Ministers in England to date have been teachers.)

This generic leadership approach, whilst sharing some common traits of what makes a good leader, does not address what makes a good school leader. Leadership of schools should not become an imitation of the corporate world with 'data dashboards' presented as the be-all and end-all for the performance of the school. It is hard to justify what great learning there is if you are only concerned with staff performance which is underpinned with evaluative qualitative (lesson observation) data but is then 'transformed' as quantitative data.

Effective schools provide great care for children and proactively take steps to have an understanding of the context of the students outside of school. This enables earlier intervention and support. Strong parental and home interaction with the school does help the children in their engagement with school and thus their attitude to learning and their achievement.

Leading a great school is fantastic. Whilst it may feel thankless and lonely for much of your time at the helm of a school or schools, the self-belief that you are shaping the way for the next generation in society should not be understated. It also becomes a source of solace and comfort in the sadly all-too-frequent moments of challenge.

Whilst you may be bogged down in the 4Bs of school management (two of which are discussed in this book): Bells, Buses, Buildings and Budgets. You may also feel far removed from the 4Cs of 21st century skills: Critical thinking, collaboration, communication and creativity, [38] which are further extended to what some called the 4Cs of 22nd century education: Culture, connectivity, (both of which are classed as 21st century by some) and also care and community. [39]

Certainly, as the world comes out of various restrictions and 'lockdowns' because of the COVID-19 pandemic, the need for care, community and connectivity are very real. School leaders must apply these same skills of being creative and collaborative to communicate ways to ensure the wellbeing of the whole school community is addressed. This is more relevant now to avoid any stigmatising of a cohort as the 'COVID-generation'.

Schools are the most vibrant, energised place in society. As a school leader, take great professional pride in the role you are fulfilling!

T

Thought leadership

The internet has distributed knowledge so openly now that you can spend your whole working day reading articles, watching videos and hopefully being inspired. The great school leaders are thought leaders. They tend to be less risk-averse and have ideas worth sharing.[40] This is what separates the good school leaders from the great school leaders. Make the effort to look beyond your school, your organisation. Consider implications for the sector.

This may not happen immediately. Not everyone can become a champion of a particular cause overnight, but if you want to aspire to become a great school leader, think ahead, have a future focus and learn from issues in the past. Take an interest in timelines too. These provide the history and progress but also enable a vision or target to aim towards. Such timelines provide journeys and the concept of the direction of travel becomes more relevant. It also allows you to organise your thoughts and plans with clarity and milestones.

For example, consider the history of education in England. Schools often began as religious institutions and often for poor boys only. The curriculum was composed of subjects which were limited to a handful of themes. (Ironically, these institutions dedicated to educating the chosen poor, in many instances, became the 'elite' schools of today!) Then these schools evolved to primary and secondary education over the past hundred and fifty years and then into tertiary education, with many universities emerging as academic powerhouses in the last hundred years.

Or consider the development of technology in schools. From the overhead projector to the interactive whiteboard and now streaming devices in the classroom. What was once the mainstay of well-resourced schools to have IT suites in each department or an IT 'block' in each school is now the mainstream for most classes to have devices such as tablets and laptops.

By having an active interest in a theme, education-related or otherwise, it helps keep your own interest and even research into becoming more than an opinion. This passion can be from the amateur to becoming the expert in the field such as Patrick Moore did in his passion for astronomy.

When invited to share your practice and insight, whilst presenting at conferences, or in discussion in seminars or when writing articles or blogs, do have a determination to offer foresight by asking questions that you intend to answer in the coming weeks and months.

Look at the 'big picture' and apply in your context even as a pilot project. By implementing something (unique) in your school, it allows further questions to be asked. Ask the big questions. As I have. My own question is why are there half a billion illiterate children? What can I do about it? In response to my self-reflection, I founded a not-for-profit organisation dedicated to eradicating global childhood illiteracy called 'All Children Read'.[41]

Why are 100% of the children not achieving the higher grades? After five or six or seven years in your school, why are there still such disparities? We know a lot more about neurodiversity, so how is the curriculum and teaching being modified to accommodate this and facilitate the progress for those needing extra support? Is it due to an 'excuses' culture? What equitable provision/earlier intervention was/was not provided and why?

Technology

Many school leaders delegate the task of technology (tech, EdTech) to the Head of IT or a new title such as Director of Technology, or even confuse matters by designating a title such as 'Innovation Lead'. Part of the reason due to a skills deficiency that some school leaders have in terms of digital literacy. In other instances, it may be due to the lack of time in being able to focus in this area and therefore by developing a leader in the school, you actually develop capacity. A small minority of leaders may perceive such a role as an administration task and add it to a task for the Data Manager or Exams Officer.

However, as the recent Covid-19 pandemic exposed the variance of remote/distance learning provision in schools, many school leaders have failed to keep up to date with the latest developments in technology. One such example is the misquote where (experienced) senior leaders refer to 'computers' (as in the fixed location PC of the 1990s), when they ought to refer to them as 'devices' such as tablets, mobile phones and laptops in this digital era. This is as much outmoded as references to decades-old computer software are included in the new Brexit agreement.[42]

Rather than 'EdTech', I prefer to call this 'technology for learning'. (TfL, akin to Assessment for Learning, AfL, as opposed to Transport for London!) I believe this provides a purpose for the technology as 'EdTech' can be too generic as anything associated with education when we ought to focus on learning.

Technology in most schools is a given. The 'Smart School' may be a theoretical utopia of a paperless school with big data and the use of artificial intelligence. Perhaps we should not be striving towards this either. The more (big) tech we allow into our schools, the more we risk the safeguard of our data. This is like a software app update on your phone when you quickly scroll down and "accept" only to realise twelve hours later, on social media, that the app can access your personal data and worse sell it to other entities with nefarious intent.

However, how we use technology and what it is used for are the key implementation questions that school leaders must take ownership of rather than delegate. Yet preceding this is to ask why we need a particular technology solution.

One of the biggest mistakes is to apply tech (usually) from a previous setting or via a friend of a friend and not understand the context of the school. This copy and paste model (excuse the pun) often means that the school is adapting to technology but rather it ought to be the other way around. The technology should be adapted for the (unique context of the) school and made bespoke rather than a generic (off the shelf) tool applied to the school, which must adjust to implement the technology. What I mean by bespoke, is not simply changing the background to match the school colours and a logo in the corner when staff sign into a particular digital platform.

I recall an IT manager in a school I joined, who was inducting me as a new staff member on a system where staff signed in using an app. I suggested "perhaps turn on location settings," and he replied, "we are a school not a prison!" This is a great example of a culture of trust and transparency not of suspicion and secrecy. Little surprise then the school was thriving and rated 'outstanding'. Shame on me!

The more effective school leaders would not expect a task to be done that they could not do or at least have an active interest and working knowledge of. These are the next generation of school leaders who are digital natives. Combining this with data science and being data literate enables you to be an architect and advocate of technology to enhance school systems and provide meaningful experiences for student learning.

In terms of skills for the future, the ability to 'learn, unlearn and relearn'[43] is going to be an essential aspect needed for adults and children alike. The pace of change with technological advances and increased access to data and information will result in one approach to learning being amended or even replaced due to a change in the physical and virtual infrastructure around us. This is the perfect methodology of authentic lifelong learning. At present, what many people assert as 'lifelong learning', is actually continuous learning (using the same methods from previous learning stages/qualifications).

Time management
So as a leader, everyone wants to meet you and you want to meet everyone! A dozen e-mails an hour and appointments with parents and meetings with staff all within a day. However, there are never enough hours in a day!

Thought leadership, Technology, Time management

A 'typical' school leader's day will be 12 hours whether this is 6am-6pm or 7am-7pm. Then upon returning home after 9pm, the messages on your phone keep coming and you keep replying and so it goes on throughout the night. By working in this manner, you extend your day into the evening and weekends and school 'holidays' but also set a dangerous precedent of an 'always on' culture, for colleagues, but also parents if you respond to their e-mails at night. This culture can then seep into the classroom by way of the teachers in their use of digital classroom apps and setting 'assignments for the next day (but going live the night before).

As such, this provides alerts and notifications to the students who on their devices may choose to message/contact the teacher on the app and so the teacher-student communication (about learning) continues late into evening or at night. Be sure to have policies in place to protect staff, parents and students with an Acceptable IT use inc devices, apps etc. to counter this 'always on' culture.

Whilst efficiency is key for the healthy work-life balance, the main issue is the psychological barrier. (Refer to Chapter W.) How much time is spent (wasted?) on matters you feel you need to be involved with or respond to? A lot of inefficiency arises from what has been lost in the day causing you to have to stay back and respond to e-mails etc.

Before you plan your week ahead, ask yourself these pertinent questions:

- What are you hoping to achieve each day?
- How much time do you spend with the students and parents each day?
- Is your diary inundated with meetings?
- Do you allow a respite time between meetings?
- Are the meetings productive?
- Are they with a formal agenda or an informal chat? (Both have merits, but often the formal becomes informal or even worse the informal is followed up with a formal e-mail in a duplicitous and callous manner and what could be seen as a

breach of trust.)

A common mistake made by staff especially when switching from teaching to leadership and management is that your digital diary can be booked up quite easily based on available 'free' slots.

When you were a main scale teacher, your day was managed for you as much as it was for the students. You are "free Period 3, but otherwise a full day". Or you "have a free (period) first thing on Thursday" etc.

Yet now in the leadership diary, yes, you may have meetings with staff based on the school timetable hours, but the chances are other 'corporate' meetings, with outside agencies such as universities, other schools and government entities will be on the hour or half-hour rather than at the start of Period 5!

Ensure what needs to be done is done that day. Block off time to respond to e-mails etc. What you want to achieve in the day is another matter. Allow time for this also.

The ideal scenario is to have achieved all you wanted to do in that day within the working day! Aim for that as an ideal by removing some meetings, shortening others, combining meetings with others in attendance to address collective or multiple issues in one meeting. Have that break between meetings to allow for overrun but also to ensure your next meeting starts on time.

U

Understanding

Knowing something, but understanding facts, people, places is a deeper level which will provide a firm foundation for you as a leader. 'Joining the dots' is what sets apart the great from the good. Whilst it is great to know about all aspects of the school, the topic etc. In reality, there will be gaps in your knowledge. The worst thing a leader can do is guess and try to plug this gap with unverified information.

It is not about what you know, but rather what you do not know. There is no shame it not knowing, but rather the shame is in not trying to find out and ask someone who does know to help fill the gap of knowledge.

The quest to seek knowledge is the pinnacle of a learner attitude. As a leader, to demonstrate this need to find out and not be expected to have all the answers all the time. The insincere leader is the one who pretends to have all the answers, usually reinforced with verbal confidence (that is often found in a used car sales representative). Such pretence leads to diminished returns further in the term when what you said as a truth was proven to be made up!

Gain that understanding through experience, reading upon a subject, consulting others, asking for demos, feedback from pilot studies etc. In the same way that you develop to understand facts, systems and the meaning behind something, be aware of understanding people in front of you.

The inexperienced school leader tends to avoid understanding people, but rather knows them only. By which I mean, they know their function in the school, what they are expected to do almost as a theoretical exercise with human resources. However, understanding people, requires effort, time and high levels of emotional intelligence, is the key to being an effective leader.

Understand what motivates a particular staff member. Understand what their context within their team dynamics is, but also outside of school. What interests or activities help shape the person who is a member of staff in the school? This will lead to improved management of people and hopefully, better motivated staff and therefore better experiences for students.

With understanding, there should be an expected level of duty of care. A way to understand is to have time to reflect but also follow up with individuals. It is too easy to have an 'open door' policy, meet new staff or you as the new leader, meet all staff and follow up if you need something from them. However, follow up a few months later to see how they are settling in their role or how the job is going for them.

Umbrella

Schools are by default, a hub for multi-service coordination. Whether this is in the form of a Multi-Agency Support Team (MAST) or a Team Around the Child (TAC) meeting, it allows other 'smaller' parties to have a voice, access and interaction with other significant entities in this umbrella format.

In the shade of this umbrella, as a school leader, you are offering protection and a much-needed voice or a platform. This could be a carer to speak about an issue, or a specialist staff member to provide an update to others who may not have had the opportunity to hear from such an individual had this forum not taken place.

As a school leader, be eager to host, coordinate and offer the school as a platform. There are mutual benefits in doing so. Firstly, it raises the profile of the school, or confirms the high status of a school. Secondly, it helps develop your profile 'outside of the school' which essentially builds your professional network, but also takes your professional learning into other domains. It allows you to develop credibility too in other areas not 'usually' seen under the auspices of a school leader.

By having the school as the umbrella, a hub and partnerships are formed. A lot of these umbrella events happen outside of the school day. These could be community events; local sports or arts clubs working in partnership with the school. By attending, promoting and supporting these events, you also increase your presence and authority in the community.

Partnership building and maintaining is a key aspect of broadening the scope of a school leader. Succession planning and delegation is also important as with all aspects of your role. Many such partnerships are lost once the incumbent leader moves on. This is the risk of people-based partnerships, whereas practice-based partnerships continue to thrive long after the original people have moved on.

An example I can recall is the partnership with a local university and the Initial Teacher Training (ITT) programme. Having assumed a role as Assistant Head, I was literally handed a folder with a few dates and a couple of e-mail addresses. It used to be a case of agreeing how many trainee teachers you want in the school and for which placement. Then, have the Headteacher sign it off and you as the lead contact would ensure the various departments were notified.

Yet by making the effort to visit the university on a few occasions, the partnership strengthened and the school became one of the top ten placement schools from a partnership of more than one hundred and sixty schools. In doing so, our school was invited to other strategy groups within the university.

This initial commitment raised the profile and resulted in further credibility in shaping and influencing policy around teacher training, but also around other pedagogy research.

Undertaking

Being honourable, honest and upright, in a rather dishonourable, dishonest and crooked world is a massive challenge. Having moral fortitude and giving and keeping your word as your bond really separates the profoundly great leaders from others.

If you agree to something, do not renege. If you must make a U-turn, have the decency to apologise. However, accept all the flack which will come your way, rather than make excuses, scapegoat, or find a stooge to take the fall. Like a sheet of paper, once it is torn, no matter how much glue or sticky tape is used, the tear remains.

Keep your word and find ways to make it happen if you anticipate hurdles ahead. Of course, be careful not to overpromise.

A new school leader will agree for something to happen based on assumptions of the additional authority that comes with the leadership territory e.g. a course for a staff member to attend or the purchase of a new resource only to be turned down by the Principal/Board.

Also, by not assuming, but rather checking you have the appropriate authority to decide before committing to something will enable you to save face. More importantly, it avoids you becoming unstuck if you did not make the promise in the first instance.

Of course, in the leadership realm, there is a lot of undermining or 'points scoring' on who has the final say, who apparently can veto and who signs the order. This is not a game for a sacrificial lamb, it is real, it affects children. Therefore, if you have the ultimate authority as Principal, ensure your SLT are enabled to have the delegated authority in their remit and scope to enable them to give their undertaking. If you are in SLT, discuss with the Principal to have the necessary scope as per your responsibilities to provide assurances to the team(s) you line manage.

There is nothing more demotivating for a colleague than to attend a line management meeting, but only to be told that the line manager must check (with their senior line manager) before agreeing to something. Of course, for major strategic issues and significant capital expenditure there must be a process of approvals. Yet for a resource or staff development allocation; these budgets should be appropriately delegated to line managers who are charged with 'value for money' decision-making.

V

Vocal

Courage is needed for great school leadership. Knowing when to be vocal and lead from the stage to challenge is a trait as a leader you should develop and adopt. This will enable you to address systemic issues, collective bargaining, wider social justice issues or even compensate for historic wrongs.

However, in the toolkit, it is just as important to have the wisdom to remain silent if the situation warrants it, as a matter of judgement, but bear witness and have the intent nonetheless to address injustices, in the background with a sense of urgency, rather than in the foreground vocally.

I have learned from being outspoken by choosing to challenge (years before #choosetochallenge became a trending social media hashtag) and much to my medium-term career detriment, that there is great wisdom in the private lobby rather than the public outcry.

Learning to hold your own counsel can be emotionally and psychologically challenging. Yet having that inner strength, knowing you have the intention to 'fight' for the greater good, to address the bigger picture, will help you to remain committed and steadfast.

To take a stand for others is a brave step that most of us choose to avoid in our selfish/self-centred or you may say indifferent stances, that often many career professionals take. Using people for your self-gain, but not helping others in their hour of need, is a very disingenuous practice.

This can easily be translatable to apathy, selfishness, or worse, the dark arts of politics akin to Machiavelli, whereby others standby during a crisis to see their leader fail and then seize this as an opportunity. How immoral is the world of school leadership whose practice can be so far removed from 'preaching' to the children to be honest, helpful and honourable?

History has taught us the high price of standing by and doing nothing. History also shows the opportunists who maximise their own gain, their fill in times of disruption and instability.

First, they came for the community schools (I was an academy leader) so I did not speak out, or first they came for the smaller independent schools (I was part of a large school) so I did not speak out. Then when the policy does affect you, you become so enraged and want to condemn the new policy but too little too late? Is there anyone left to speak on your behalf, or offer support?

Build alliances and a network of peers and professionals. This will enable a sense of either collective commitment or working through others, to address the ever-moving goalposts such that education is.

Vehicle

A school is the means to an end and not an end in itself. A platform for the journey. A vehicle for improvement. Education should be an opportunity to develop character and the mind, applying knowledge to make informed decisions.

Indeed, for most school leaders, education and schools as such should be a vehicle for social mobility, increased literacy and numeracy and therefore ALL school leavers should leave school with a sense of fulfilment but also tangible achievement.

As a school leader, your actions, thoughts and words have to enable this vehicle to be one for progress and not limiting life chances of any child in your supervision. This is an extremely high expectation, but one as school leaders, you should embrace fully and not see it as a challenge too difficult to meet.

When schools boast on banners on the school gate and on social media about record results e.g. 90% success rate (which is outstanding in any inspection framework by a long way) it still means 10% have not succeeded.

This deficit analysis approach does not help curb any hard-earned celebration of success but provides a timely reminder of what more is needed to ensure that ALL schools ensure achievement for ALL children in their care and supervision.

Additionally, you have a duty for the profession. The profession has enabled you to become a school leader, therefore reciprocate this for the next generation: To attract staff to the teaching profession. Train teachers, retain them, develop them and ultimately grow leaders of school communities.

Despite the various external pressures on staff and unfair comparisons with other sectors, teaching is one of the most, if not the most rewarding career. This message cannot be lost but it is often diluted in the midst of the melee of the politics and bureaucracy of schools.

Learn to steer the staff towards an optimistic pathway for their futures and in doing so it will transpire to the students.

What separates great school leaders from the good is that they do not magpie and almost out of jealousy keep all the best teachers for their own school. Instead, great leaders are confident enough to keep attracting and growing teachers and if they do 'move on' to other schools, they understand in the domain of system leadership that great teachers will want to fulfil their ambition to assume greater responsibilities and seek promotion.

Verbal reasoning

School leaders are as much a legal custodian of the organisation as they are the operational and academic gatekeepers.

Therefore, policy updates, new inspection frameworks, curriculum modifications and many other 'guidelines' will inevitably end up in your inbox or in-tray (the latter in my days!) for you to obtain a coherent understanding and usually disseminate a summary to other audiences; made up of the common five: SLT, Staff, Governors, Parents and Students.

Trawling through large electronic files and summarising the salient points is a skill – and one worth developing if you are not so keen to do so currently. Certainly, as a new school leader, avoid the need to print off the file to highlight and annotate for your own summary. In this era of digital tools, have an electronic pen, stylus or e-notes and save the cost of the paper resources and the planet respectively!

Consequently, having summarised the document, the chances are you will need to present. (Refer to Chapter P.) How often do you see presentations with dozens of lines, made of up of a paragraph copied from an official document? Often the presenter is reading them line by line verbatim or the opposite by merely skimmed through before the audience can take in any of the (excessive) detail?

As a leader, consider the audience and learn from other sectors. The 'Executive Summary' approach is what you need to develop; or if you have this skill then develop it in other team members.

Sharing a document with dozens of pages for the audience to read, whether it is e-mailed or copied into a large presentation file or worse still the original file attached does defeat the purpose of your role as an effective gatekeeper, filter and summariser. It can also come across as lazy or at best forwarding akin to social media (in which people often forward media, files without in some cases checking its validity)!

e.g. #fakenews: Here is a picture of a building wrecked in a flood; but actually, it refers to a different event a few years earlier and in a different location!

If you feel there is a verbal reasoning deficit, consider enhancing your verbal reasoning but also the two other aspects – not only are these found in many psychometric or aptitude assessments but for your own toolbox, it is important to develop competencies across the skills spectrum: spatial reasoning and quantitative reasoning.

Not only is this good for your own logic but being numerate and effective with numerical processing espouses a greater level of proficiency and sharpness needed for mental agility. As mentioned previously, do not fall into the school leader 'boast' of failure, "I failed at Maths!" Nobody would admit it is honourable to be illiterate then why is it acceptable to be innumerate?

W

Work-life balance

The demands of a school leader are such that 'work' continues 'out of hours'. Cynically put, do you ever switch off from your work? I do not think this is the correct question. Rather, do you ensure you have time outside from your work location and working day to have the capacity to refresh, reenergise and refocus? This is easier said than done. The nature of your role is such that even in 'school holidays' you have ongoing issues and tasks to attend to.

However, my advice is to avoid bringing work home. Stay back if you need to so you can leave the school and literally go home. You may say but we all have our work habits and some of us prefer to work at home. Yet if this is the case, make it the exception and not the norm. Also, you can schedule e-mails to be sent in the morning rather than 'pinging' in the inbox of colleagues.

I seldom practised this, in the past twenty years, much to my regret. Instead, I was too busy at home or outside of school, responding to e-mails, phone calls and messages. Frequently, I was looking at my device and often saying in the presence of my family and friends, "sorry, can you say that again?" as I had not paid attention to their conversation with me! I should have given them more of my focus and listened to what they had discussed in the first place! I regret being so ignorant, disrespectful, rude and 'addicted' (workaholic), filled with a sense of urgency that I felt I needed to reply to every work communication outside of work!

Furthermore, in the post-pandemic digital world, the expectation to work from home is very real in the corporate world. Yet in a school setting, we can organise our work and home life more robustly – if we choose to.

Avoid a mobile phone messaging culture too. This is not needed and only adds to another avenue of communication. It also affects the instant messaging or almost impulsive reply or the urge to reply or have a final say.

The cost and damage to your health and family is one that cannot be retrospectively rectified. Also, the very real risk of burnout or working based on fatigue and stress can lead to making erroneous decisions or at least less considered choices.

E-mails can wait.[44] What is really urgent on an e-mail? You can be called on the phone for an emergency issue assuming you are in the expected chain of command for emergency response management. There is no need to continue an e-mail thread into the evening. It also impacts on others which is the most important aspect as a leader. Your actions will resonate and how your behaviours will reflect on the team and the school community.

If you reply at 10pm others may feel the need to. Indeed, have a policy, a code of conduct or communications policy if it is a case of reshaping an unhealthy work culture. Have an out of office reply, or even if you want to, avoid having your work e-mail on your mobile phone altogether! Once others reflect the boundaries you have set for your working operations, it facilitates wellbeing for all.

Having said that it is better to avoid bringing any work home or extending the working day, it will always remain as a source of tension regarding how much of your work creeps into your personal out of work hours' time and space.

This is a state of equilibrium, which the chemistry teachers reading this will understand, is affected by temperature, pressure and concentration. (Le Châtelier's principle.[45]) Similarly, the work-life balance is as much based on managing priorities dependent on the same factors as studied in chemistry. How you manage these will determine the work-life balance. They are all in one way a sense of prioritising. What can wait until the next working day, or later in the week (or term) and what needs responding to in the same day:

- **Temperature:** *i.e. how urgent is something?*

Is it deadline dependent and needs resolving according by a particular time or date? Examples include calendar-related deadlines such that impact reports, events and information needed to be published.

- **Pressure:** *i.e. how important is something?*

Communication from or a response needed to which authority? Does this particular task warrant a higher level of prioritising? An inspection body or safeguarding authority may well need a higher response than perhaps a request from another school for some information.

- **Concentration:** *i.e. how much volume of work?*

Can it be managed at a later date or is it such that it needs clearing before you leave school site? These could be operational matters which are site-dependent or if a 'high concentration' such as procurement requests, lesson observation schedule and feedback to staff or responding to dozens of new e-mails in your inbox. Finding the time in the working day to see to these can prove to be a challenge. Therefore, consider blocking time off in your working day with a 'Do Not Disturb' notice to resolve these matters rather than having to stay back and 'tidy up'.

Yet you must ensure enough space to be refreshed and energised. Eating healthily, exercising regularly and where possible switching off are all vital for your commitment, effectiveness and longevity in school leadership.

Why?

Curiosity should remain with school leaders. That sense of wonder. Why is this happening or why is this not happening?! Can we do this better? Can we do it differently? Can we be more productive, more efficient? Can we improve further? Some ask why? As a leader, remind to ask yourself why not?[46] As a School Leader, you need to not only question what is around you, what you have inherited, or what others tell you, but also for all your own actions start with the Why?[47] From the why, you can then move onto the how and find solutions, improvement, or new ways to adapt and amend or adopt and implement.

Existential questions: Why are you a school leader? Why did you become a teacher? To make a difference? To have a successful career? To provide better opportunities for others? How are you going to achieve this? What has worked well in your career to date and what has not?

Performance questions: Why isn't this teacher performing well in class? How can you ensure all teachers are mentored, coached and supported so there is a consistent high performance across the school?
Why are those staff always late for deadlines? Do they not value the framework being presented? Are they not motivated?

Why are these students not making progress? Or at the other end of the scale, why are these students making above expected progress? Is it due to great teaching, other support outside of school or strong neurological development? How have you used or enabled others to use data more effectively to make an evidence-based analysis of the student attainment and progress? What has been done previously that proved to be effective or ineffective? What changes are needed? When should you commence any intervention? Who should lead on this?

Operational questions: Why is there a backlog of students going through a corridor or stairwell? For example, I have visited many schools where in a building entrance or corridor opening, only one door is open (in a double doorway. Yet for the past x years the same congestion on the stairwells and corridors remains as nobody appears to have asked why? If they have, they have not followed up with a solution i.e. open the other door! It can make a lot of difference especially with social distancing requirements during the recent pandemic.

Why is there so much litter? Are there enough bins, or do students not care about their school community? Have you engaged with the student voice/student council to have environmental initiatives? Could you lead by example and do a litter pick? Or do you feel (it is beneath you and) it is "not your job".

Stakeholder questions: Why are these parents behaving this way? What are the dynamics of the parent body? Has this changed over time?

Strategic questions: Why are the students from a particular feeder school or locality performing better than other students of a 'similar' ability? What outreach and support programmes can be devised to address this cohort variance?

Wins

Celebrate the quick wins. As a new leader, credibility is something that needs to be earned along with respect from colleagues. You cannot assume nor expect the community you are leading to be 'on your side' from the outset merely due to your title or office. (Nor should you ever expect to be given respect because of your position, but rather earn the respect over time as you settle into your role.)

As mentioned throughout this book, I advise you to spend around 100 days (or the first term), reviewing, reflecting and taking note of what is working well and what could be improved, enhanced, or changed. However, that does not mean that your 'impact' will only happen after this.

School leadership, as mentioned earlier in this book, is a lonely job at times and the win can be a sense of relief as much as a sense of achievement. Impact, recognition and celebration of staff or students can be in public as much as it can be personal. The win of others being recognised by you or others recognising what you have achieved does provide positivity which will resonate in the school community.

Wins are not necessarily tangible. Wins can easily shape into motivation and build momentum. Yet wins can be less tangible but equally or more fruitful. Wins such as the presence of mind, emotional intelligence in building relations with colleagues and the rapport with students and parents is also immensely beneficial.

Wins will happen for you as it will occur for other staff. Facilitating the wins for other staff is not only magnanimous, but it gives credit to your colleagues and is a real win for you. Motivated colleagues will work better and be more effective and feel a sense of commitment and belonging.

The great thing about 'wins,' is that it creates a culture of winning and it can go on to lead to further success and a 'can do' belief, where it may have previously been lacking.

An example from my experience is implementing a leading tech company infrastructure with the certification of competency to accompany this. A few teachers who were 'early adopters' obtained this 'official' certification and went on to become 'champions' and advocates, ambassadors for this technology platform.

Yet the feeling of success enabled staff who were 'tech-averse' to engage and their sense of achievement in also becoming a certified educator was really felt amongst the school community. This became such that even non-teaching staff went on to obtain this certification as a belief in its merit for enhancing digital literacy and the culture of success spread across the school community.

Yet be sincere in giving credit where it is due. Is it an actual win? This is the key to ensure it is genuine. Too often praise is issued for an 'expected' achievement and this devalues the win worth celebrating or an accomplishment based on normal expectations. "A big thank you for completing the reports on time". It could be 'a dig' at those who have not completed on time, but it does also lessen the effect of saying 'Thank You' in future.

For example, a genuine 'thank you' for the site staff who regularly stayed back (as you stayed back late into the evening) to lock up the building in the evening or any other 'unsung' heroes, who often go out of their way beyond their 'job description' is worthy of recognition.

X

X-ray vision

We do not have comic book fictional superhero powers (though I think some school leaders do feel invincible!) However, as school leaders or any team leader, you need to be able to see through others, see through the spin and make sure what lies beneath is healthy. The pretentious or hidden agenda can divert valuable time and resources into addressing things that are not the priorities now.

This ability to see through any pretentious or hidden agenda, is not only for people management. The ability to extend your thinking to see ahead and develop foresight is also an essential tool for an effective leader.

See all staff in front of you, but have vision, see what is beyond the school. As I said to the students of all my Year 11 classes in my final lesson farewell speech, "look out of the window. If you can see the trees, you can see, but if you can see beyond the trees and see the world for what it can offer, you have vision".

Staying with the medical theme, having a forensic approach with a mastery memory or a clinical touch really helps with spotting things from afar. This may be 20-20 vision rather than X-ray (and you may be correct in your thinking that this topic should be under 'V' for Vision)!

Such abilities separate the best leaders from the very good. Some leadership traits that you may have or learn to acquire will be in the realm of aiming for perfection, the 100% mindset; for if you believe every child can achieve, then you must have that totality, completion in your thinking. This will lead to accusations of being pedantic, 'nit-picky' or obsessed with the small details such as becoming a 'traffic warden' for SPaG (Spelling and Grammar).

I have received many 'parking tickets' from the SPaG traffic wardens in my time, though I could not put it down to being an EAL pupil and learning English fluently around the age of 7 years old! I recall in my third year of teaching; I was presenting to a council cabinet. It was an interactive session on our school's VLE (Virtual Learning Environment) showcasing anytime anywhere learning. A couple of Year 8 students were also in attendance as 'live' learners. When it came to the 'question and answer' plenary session, the only points raised by a councillor were: "login is not a verb but a noun" and that the "textbox is not highlighted but filled" (I had said to the students, can you log in please, but spelt it as login and referred to some highlighted text, but it was a filled textbox apparently?!)

I know I have often made the error throughout this book as many schools do, to spell 'Headteacher', or 'Principal' as proper nouns, when it ought to be head teacher (as two words) or principal, being grammatically correct as per the English language!

In a similar 'eagle-eyed' approach, many schools are more concerned about image and branding. Whilst marketing is important to attract students to your school, it is important to remain mission-aligned to the aims of your school. If the branding cannot bring value to the students' learning experience or climate in the school, then it ought not to be considered. How much is spent on new websites, new signage, new school uniform?

Often such rebranding is a vain attempt to relaunch a school's image. Some have worked, but many have failed as expensive gimmicks and have incurred additional cost needlessly (from parents' income, indirectly from tax if a public (government state) school or directly from their income if a fee-paying private school) and hundreds of hours of effort spent which have detracted the leadership and management from the core purpose of the school: to provide better life opportunities for the children/students.

Exception

(I know this contains an 'X', but such is the challenge of the English language with letters starting with X!)

To be consistent is key. However, by default there are exceptions in the context. Remember when you were a (full-time) teacher. If the student's book was genuinely damaged and the student was unable to complete the homework on time, would an allowance be made?

Scale this up to managing staff who were unable to meet a deadline.
If it is a recurring theme, that is different, but the context should be considered. The teacher with perhaps domestic responsibilities i.e. carer for elderly parents or having young children or marital challenges vs a colleague with no responsibilities living on their own are not alike. The 'additional' time that teachers often must commit to, outside their working day is excessive, despite the best intentions to curtail it by Government or Governors! Hence the time demand vs available time will vary for each member of staff depending on their context.

Making exceptions is on a case-by-case basis. It requires judgement and no amount of training can prepare you for this. It will certainly develop your inner resolve and having a good basis of emotional intelligence and compassion will stand you in good stead.

Where exceptions become the norm i.e. a staff member can leave early on a particular day for the whole year; then it must be addressed within a policy framework to avoid cries of favouritism, inconsistent treatment, or bias.

The exception is there for others, but not for you. As a school leader, be consistent. Demonstrate great organisation, punctuality, follow up/feedback and application of policy without privilege. As mentioned before in the topic on 'Hypocrisy,' any well-earned credibility built over months can be ruined in a day based on perception or actual hypocrisy nearing nepotism or self-indulgence.

A great manager can manage exceptions for their team and cohort. A great leader has the skillset to be agile in uncertain times and ensure the team cross the line in a cohesive manner. It may not be altogether, but all members of the team are able to achieve their aims with support where needed.

Axe to grind

Avoid the risk to carry out vendettas against the staff who may have been your obstruction in the past. This is especially applicable to internal promotions to SLT or Headship. This can take away your professionalism as it appears personal. It also takes away focus on why you became a teacher and you use up energy on planning, plotting and almost drowning in your bitterness.

This trait is early on in your teaching career. That 'annoying' student who was rude to you or spent weeks disrupting your well-planned lessons. You become incensed and lower expectations and 'ensure that student fails' as your last say in the matter. After failing the student, you then say "well, what do you expect? The student was always going to fail as (s)he had a poor attitude to learning".

The cycle of bitterness continues and in doing so you have broken the unwritten and unspoken oath in the profession – that all children should be afforded the chance to succeed. Is it really the child's fault? Was it the activity that made the student bored? Are they from a dysfunctional household with minimum parental/guardian support? This vindictive trait can also eat into any leadership development.

How you manage staff often stems from how you have been managed or how you have supervised students when you were a full-time teacher. Do you have any favouritism or bias (unconscious or intentional)? Do you have any prejudice? Are you micro-aggressive? Are you dismissive? Are your communication methods and content passive-aggressive (especially in e-mails, always wanting to have the last say)?

You will have some people (staff, parents, or students) who will have riled you over the years, or if joining a new school, in the first month. This could be that staff member who ignores your deadlines or goes to another colleague or jumps to the Principal, your line manager (if you are SLT) for a second opinion.

Or it could be that parent who verbally abuses you and calls you out (falsely) because they are so angry about their perceived unfair treatment. It could be the defiant student, who disobeys your instruction, to put the chewing gum in the bin or remove the hat inside the school building (speaking from my experience), only for the student to comply with a more junior (but established) member of staff such as a Head of Year or Head of House.

By having scores to settle, it detracts from your purpose and role. You need to have broad shoulders to carry this and move on and have a thick skin and not let this get to you no matter how demeaning it may be.

Similarly, with staff you cannot be expected to be 'friends' with everyone, but rather be friendly as they are focused on the same mission. Being agreeable does not mean you have to agree to everything, but a great leader is tolerant of other views, approaches without bearing a grudge, so long as achievement for **all** children, is not jeopardised.

Y

Yes people

Leaders do not need to be popular, but they need to do what is right for the greater good, the strategic priorities rather than to please people. In doing so, they will do what is right for all children in their care and consequently for all staff.

New leaders often feel the need or want to seek tacit approval. There is often a risk of wanting to please others and say the right things that the audience wants to hear as opposed to doing the right thing.

An example is a Middle Leader running a CPD session with their friends in attendance for implicit support. If you are a new school leader resulting from an internal promotion, the risk of your friends whom you have worked alongside for many years becoming a clique and nodding to your every word is very real. How to avoid this? Make a point of sitting away from your 'friends' and actually have mixed group 'seating plans' if it is a staff professional learning session so cliques cannot sit with one another.

Another example of cliques is that of parents. Usually parent governors or parent councils/associations. Whilst they may be the fans of the school and your leadership; it does risk giving a lop-sided view of the world according to parents. This is also another avenue to ensure you have a balanced view of the parent body. Surveys do not always work as the ones that love and equally the ones that loathe the school tend to complete the survey with positive and negative feedback accordingly.

The silent 'middle' majority (as per a normal distribution curve) are the ones whose views you should try to obtain. How? Invite such parents who have not previously volunteered or complained to attend a breakfast or lunch with you (work commitments not withstanding); this gives a necessary platform for such parents.

They could be parents of younger or older students, parents of a particular cohort of students according to gender, race, poverty, or academic ability, which helps provide a perspective on what support is being offered or what more is needed or what is working well in the school-home partnership.

Leaders by the function of the name and title need followship. This can happen alongside fellowship (with peers, colleagues and work friends) but it should not be because of. You do not need to seek this affection. You do not need yes people. It stems from an insecurity deep within, that affirmation is needed for every key action or communication.

As a new school leader, you will naturally be more aware of your shortcomings and the strive for perfection will be there. Avoid issues such as having to reprint documents (if you still work in a school obsessed with paper handouts in this era of sustainability awareness!) or having to please a certain audience who thought the 'presentation was excellent,' when many staff misunderstood the key message and follow-up meetings are needed. Some are valid amendments, such as the need to send a follow-up e-mail to correct any errors in the previous message i.e. "further to my previous email, the actual time for the session is…"

This could be due to carelessness of not checking your initial e-mail or a rushed message sent without the necessary drafting/checking (usually because the modern practitioner has adopted an 'instant messenger' mindset and impulsively sends or replies to e-mails via the mobile phone).

However, the ones who are more hostile to you or more averse are the ones to bring on board; the detractors and the laggards are the ones who you ought to pay more attention to.

As you grow in your role, the challenge to please all people will be ever present. Have a transparent approach to the treatment of all staff and take the challenge and critique from colleagues as a welcome feedback, rather than seeking public affirmation.

The need for affirmation is to be afforded but in the privacy of line management and SLT meetings, you can have an agreed approach where approval is needed or sought. This will give you the confidence to proceed with the wider audience whether this is staff, parents, or students.

Youthful

Why did you become a teacher? Most will say: "to make a difference" or the "love of their subject area". I would say one of the greatest privileges of working in schools is being motivated to help fulfil the ambitions of the children and by doing so, having the 'Peter Pan syndrome' of never wanting to grow up!

Each new academic year brings a new cohort and a rejuvenation, with the innocence of youth. This is something quite unique in schools and the new arrivals by default, bring their energy, hopes and wishes in front of all the teachers and other staff each year!

This energy should transfer to you as a school leader, an almost emotional fountain of youth to keep you focused in helping find solutions for these students for their futures. It is not only a case of choosing the right curriculum and portfolio of qualifications, but rather ensuring the 'hidden curriculum' is just as successful in ensuring the character and confidence of the students along with dozens of other skills are firmly developed.

The children become adolescents and young adults. The youth are indeed the hope for the next generation and should be encouraged to do great things in the community whilst in school and contribute to society at large, upon completing school.

Every year a new cohort enter and so the cycle of childhood to adulthood development continues. This is a great opportunity to allow not only you, but your team, your colleagues to also tap into this rejuvenation process on an annual basis!

The journey from childhood to adolescence should also remind you that despite any major challenges, setbacks or even (perceived) 'disasters' in the school year, the journey of the child continues. Use this as the pathway and they will get to their destination (to use a travel analogy).

In the process of being youthful, the 'Humour' and 'Joy' mentioned in previous topics, can come to fruition readily. The warmth that a school should have with praise for the efforts, attitudes and achievements of the students enhance child and youth brain development. The silent walk in the corridor or work in silence (that I certainly experienced with some teachers despite it not being an exam session!) is not a natural disposition for humans. The fear (of authority, being bullied etc.) and the 'shutdown' directives have been proven to be detrimental to neurological development.[48]

So, as you remain youthful or grow old gracefully, remember the youth in front of you, remember your own childhood and take these moments as strength to remain at your optimum self, with and for the children.

Yesterday

Look back to go forward. As you grow in your role, key milestones will be met and this will help as a reference point in navigating your journey. Learn from mistakes but also preserve successful strategies from the past. School leaders tend to conform and mitigate risk. By being risk averse, mistakes are seldom made due to the lack of risks taken.

However, whenever a mistake occurs, from an intentional risk or new strategy or a general oversight, make a note of it. Do not blame others and take responsibility for the (unintended) outcome. Have a mental or psychological repository as well as a physical or digital archive. It enables you to avoid reinventing the wheel, but it also prevents you having to drive with a flat tyre over that speed bump!

As a new school leader, no doubt you will plan to move ahead into the future and march "onwards and upwards" as a CEO once said to me. However, the retrospect, benefit of hindsight can ensure you avoid the mind traps and pitfalls from the past or previous roles you have held.

At the other end of the 'scale,' you are 'only as good as the last game' is an important message to heed. Do not be fixated on past glories achieved yesteryear. Of course, these help build your legacy, but often the tried and tested becomes the stagnated (over time).

It is important to review and reflect on successful actions carried out in the past, but ensure they are modified to reflect the present era. Having a mental archive is also a good reference point but, in this era, (having previously decried too much device time in this book) take a photo or add a voice or digital note.

An example I came across was a teacher in an 'outstanding' school in England, who had outstanding results in the classroom. He only changed the year date on the worksheet, as he methodically went through the same scheme of work for more than twenty years. This may have 'worked' in a pre-internet and digital era, but now with methods of learning require skills to be refined. The techniques of rote learning and content absorption fall short of the holistic outcomes needed in this modern era.

Furthermore, if the aim of such pedagogy was for successful exam preparation, the old days of the teacher issuing the past papers according to their revision schedule falls short, as past papers can be accessed online, with solutions.

(I have also experienced this same pedagogy as an undergraduate at university with a few tutors, whose lecture notes had the date from five years previously!)

As a school leader, ensure the whole workforce is future-focused. Take staff out of their comfort zones in some professional development opportunities and allow them to 'think ahead' and discuss and even design the classroom of the future.

Z

Zeal

Keep reminding yourself of why you are in the role. School leadership is not for everyone. By default, you have stood out from others to have assumed this role: To make a positive difference to the lives of hundreds if not thousands of children is one of the biggest privileges you can have; and to grow and develop staff is also a bonus for sure.

Of course, the contrary is true, get it wrong and you have ruined a generation in that community, but having the zeal to believe and do what is right in providing life-changing opportunities for hundreds of teenagers whether it be a set of worthwhile qualifications or in developing a mindset for lifelong learning will ensure your zeal has shone through to enable these students to succeed.

It is not an 'all about you' way i.e. 'look at me' on social media sharing photos of kids holding certificates of great exam results or you stood in front of the school building with an 'outstanding' rated inspection report. Rather it is really 'about you' . . . and what you do and how you do things and when you do things; that means all your actions, words and even thoughts need to be measured and applied in context.

Zeal should not be conflated with ego or emotions. Saying or doing in a reactive way just because you can in your role with the authority you possess will have longer-term negative consequences.

Learn to put the role and personality to one side and rather lead by being a 'guide from the side'.[49] To facilitate, rather than dominate, to enable others rather than direct colleagues is one of the most rewarding aspects of school leadership.

Zeal is at the heart of it. Your passion for learning, enhancing children's life opportunities and supporting staff will be evident. A great school leader inspires others. A great school manager ensures others do the job very well but will lack those awe-inspiring moments such as when communicating with colleagues.

However, school leaders also need to be inspired. The zeal found in others can resonate within you too. You need to be inspired as well as inspire others. It is too easy to be looking at your context in your part of the world in your time, rather than looking far and beyond.

Look across the globe for current inspiring leaders within education and beyond. Also study historical figures for examples of leadership, behaviours and actions and the consequences of these. Examples of great legacies but also those on the opposite end, we can learn just as much on how not to do things i.e. dictatorial.

Lastly, by having zeal, I mean have a passion for education, but do not become a zealot! Do not become a leader where your world view is the only one that is valid! A difference of opinion, a break from the consensus and respectfully agreeing to disagree exists for a reason, to prevent narrow-mindedness.

Zone

There are three areas to discuss under this heading:

Firstly, being in and out of your comfort zone. Leadership should be about leading the way, which by its very nature means you will be at the forefront of change, challenge and choices. This will put you out of your comfort zone. Sometimes this is down to being in 'uncharted territory' and therefore not knowing how to navigate; other times, it is about the potential loss of authority, even momentarily, as you seek to find out and reassert yourself in this new context. I would argue on the other hand that management is about maintaining the successful methods, customs and practice, which means remaining in your comfort zone.

Yet being out of your comfort zone, occasionally rather than ordinarily, may not be good for stress levels, but it does enable new ways of thinking, with new or alternative solutions to issues that have arisen. It also provides an organic opportunity for others to collaborate and becomes a very developmental experience, with no 'right answers' but rather 'a draft response'. The recent pandemic is a great example of this.

Schools have had to work within their teams to find solutions for safe operating of schools to incorporate social distancing and online learning provision. Yet it has also enabled schools to work across the sector to find solutions, whether this is which technology platform to use; how to host virtual parent-teacher meetings or how to modify the classroom for a safe return.

Secondly 'in the zone'. Leadership can easily become territorial, but it does require focused time too. This focus enables a high performance, which is expected from you. The 'Do Not Disturb' e-mail notification or sign on your door, whilst annoying to others, is a useful way to ensure your expected task is completed in the allocated timeslot in your diary. This requires discipline to ensure your workflow is not interrupted. You can literally block off the day twice or three times to respond to e-mails, rather than feeling compelled to reply instantly with the 'ping' notification of a new e-mail in your inbox.

Consider having 'blocked off' time in the week for thinking and reflection too. Even half an hour a week to make notes, reflect on last week's notes and thoughts of what went well and why and how could something be further improved.

This may be contrary to the 'open door' policy that many great leaders have. However, as I can certainly testify, this open door becomes more like a revolving door to your office with different people discussing matters with you all the time in the working day. The net result is you 'begin' your work after the school day and either take it home with you or stay back into the evening at school to complete all your necessary tasks for that day. This is not healthy and it will wear you down and thus impact your own performance.

Thirdly, Vygotsky's zone of proximal development[50] or zonal proximity. Effective teachers learn how to develop students to master a skill or activity or concept by gradually withdrawing the direct intervention. Effective school leaders develop staff into managers to perform tasks without needing to be told to, but also into leaders who are solution-focused and driven for success.

Zenith

Now this advice is saved for the very last chapter for a reason. The previous topics were indeed a guide for new leaders.

Now having achieved your aims and objectives, (and you are no longer a new leader but rather an established leader), consider moving on assuming you have built a strong foundation for succession planning. Sometimes, it is too easy to be settled in one place, but even if you do not intend to move on, grow the next generation of leaders to enable them to move on and lead schools as well . . . or even better than you have.

The insecure school leader literally takes their SLT with them (much like a travelling circus and the new ringmaster in town?).

A great school leader is not blighted by pride nor blinded by ambition but can know what has been achieved and any further tenure will have little further impact other than to maintain the great outcomes.

More so, great leaders 'grow leaders'. With effective systems established and succession planning, schools that are built by architects[6] (not literally the ones that design the building, but the school leaders who shape and design the ethos, beliefs and values of the school) go on to have a culture that develops as a legacy and new leader(s) step up into this.

Moving on, up or across depending on your context should not be a selfish choice, but rather a right choice. I say 'moving across', as system leadership is a term that has become more popular in the last decade, coinciding with the rise of cross-regional multi-academy trust or clusters of schools. Having led one school very well, could you reach a new zenith in leading across schools to have systems that support more than one school?

Similarly, it is not always about being at your peak, or past your peak in one school, but wanting to achieve more in a different context. A new challenge. A new setting.

The initial challenge or barrier you may face is joining another successful school, where external appointments are rather difficult, as the internal candidate would assume the promotion, to provide continuity (of success for an individual school). Yet this should not be a deterring factor if you have the intent to move on.

The other thing to consider, for a school leader is when to step aside or even step down to return to main scale teaching. This should not be seen as a demotion in the ever-infringing corporate jargon creeping into schools i.e. a vertical career trajectory. To return to the classroom from the boardroom should not be seen as something that is a failure.

You may have had a decade 'at the top' and have led some great initiatives in schools, but you may literally want a few years in teaching before pursuing other ambitions, or maybe a return to teaching full time in the classroom. You may also want to step aside and add value on specific aspects to the school by supporting colleagues in a coaching capacity or lead on specific projects in school development.

The challenge is knowing when to move out from your seat of leadership or from the school you are in. This is very much about reconciling your ambitions and having contentment within your heart and those close around you whom you care for and care for you.

Conclusion

Leadership is defined as leading others. This implies followship (unless you are holding their hand (in a metaphorical sense) by which I would suggest is management rather than leadership.

To enable followers, you need them to believe in you as a genuine and effective leader. Consequently, you need values that must transpire with intentions, actions and words.

By regular reflection, you learn to adapt or adopt better practice.

School leadership is one of the most rewarding roles. Despite the challenges to first secure the position, it is not a natural progression as can be found in some careers.

Being part of a Senior Leadership Team and having influence on whole school affairs is immensely satisfying. Further on in the leadership journey and assuming a Headship or Principalship is indeed the aim of many school leaders. A noble one. However, Headship can be a lonely experience akin to Football Management in terms of 'finger pointing'.

No doubt you will have your own A-Z list that you would like to add or certainly remove some that I included.

Ultimately, so long as you can be authentic, be the change, make the difference to the children and the future of your community, country and the world, then you can sit back and look back on your career and contribution with a great deal of fulfilment.

I end by saying "thank you" to the thousands of school leaders and teachers locally, nationally and globally who - as the recent pandemic has proved - are indeed heroes and an inspiration to the children and parents and the next generation of the world.

About the author

Kausor Amin-Ali qualified as a teacher of mathematics from the University of Cambridge. He has nearly two decades of experience working in numerous schools in England and the UAE, with twelve years in senior school leadership including Principalship, and five years as a Governor.

He has successfully completed several leadership development programmes including Fastrack Teaching, NCSL Leadership Pathways, and the Accelerate to Headship: Future Leaders. He has also obtained the National Professional Qualification for Headship (NPQH) and the National Professional Qualification for Executive Leadership (NPQEL).

As a Thought Leader, he has had various articles published, including in TES. Topics covered relate to #futureschool, assessment, digital strategy, wellbeing and social mobility.

He is also the Founder of All Children Read,[51] a global not-for-profit organisation and delivery partner dedicated to eradicating global childhood illiteracy.

ENDNOTES

[1] Waters, R. (1979) *Another Brick in the Wall part 2*. Pink Floyd Music Publishers.

[2] https://www.tes.com/news/roald-dahl-day-charlie-and-the-chocolate-factory-education-golden-ticket

[3] https://www.reference.com/world-view/origin-phrase-takes-village-raise-child-3e375ce098113bb4

[4] https://www.tes.com/news/estelle-morris-quits

[5] Ryan, W. Gilbert, I. (Ed.) (2008) *Leadership with a moral purpose*. London: Crown House.

[6] https://hbr.org/2016/10/the-one-type-of-leader-who-can-turn-around-a-failing-school

[7] Peters, T. and Waterman, R.H. (1982) *In Search of Excellence: Lessons from America's Best-Run Companies*. New York: Harper Business.

[8] Sinek, S. (2010). *How great leaders inspire action*. TED. https://www.youtube.com/watch?v=qp0HIF3SfI4

[9] Chapman, L. and West-Burnham, J. (2010) *Education for Social Justice: Achieving wellbeing for all*. London: Continuum.

[10] https://www.weforum.org/agenda/2020/10/top-10-work-skills-of-tomorrow-how-long-it-takes-to-learn-them/

[11] https://www.tes.com/magazine/article/5-ways-school-leaders-can-put-their-wellbeing-first

[12] @emileon86 Leonardi, E. Photo of poor boy sharing lollipop taken in Freetown, Sierra Leone in 2010. *Instagram*, photographed by Emil Leonardi, 27 September 2016. https://www.instagram.com/p/BK3F4jph7Ak/

[13] https://www.psychologytoday.com/us/basics/dunning-kruger-effect

[14] https://www.ted.com/talks/carol_dweck_the_power_of_believing_that_you_can_

ENDNOTES

improve

[15] Murrin, D. (2011) *Breaking the Code of History*. Hazlemere: Apollo

[16] https://www.tes.com/news/charity-school-wellbeing-lockdown-future

[17] https://simonsinek.com/product/leaders-eat-last

[18] https://www.gov.uk/government/collections/english-indices-of-deprivation

[19] https://www.gov.uk/government/news/coasting-schools-meeting

[20] Zemickis, R. and Gale B. (1985) *Back to the Future*. https://www.scripts.com/script.php?id=back_to_the_future_74&p=26

[21] https://www.tes.com/news/exams-2021-international-future-gcse-alevel

[22] Gladwell, M. (2008) *Outliers: The Story of Success*. New York: Penguin

[23] Busch, B. and Watson, E. (2019) *The Science of Learning: 77 Studies That Every Teacher Needs to Know*. Abingdon: Routledge.

[24] https://ie-today.co.uk/comment/if-you-want-to-move-forward-together-give-everyone-a-voice/

[25] https://digitalaccessforall.co.uk

[26] https://www.classtools.net/diamond9/

[27] https://www.bbc.co.uk/news/health-55620100

[28] https://dictionary.cambridge.org/dictionary/english/magpie

[29] Jones, J. (2004) *Management Skills in Schools: A Resource for School Leaders*. London: Sage.

[30] Busch, B. and Watson, E. (2019) *The Science of Learning: 77 Studies That Every Teacher Needs to Know*. Abingdon: Routledge.

[31] https://simonsinek.com/product/leaders-eat-last-book/

[32] Gladwell, M. (2008) *Outliers: The Story of Success*. New York: Penguin

[33] https://www.gov.uk/government/publications/the-7-principles-of-public-life

[34] https://simonsinek.com/product/start-with-why/

[35] https://www.tes.com/news/apple-google-microsoft-teaching-certificate-which-

ENDNOTES

is-best-why

[36] https://hbr.org/2001/01/the-making-of-a-corporate-athlete

[37] https://www.tes.com/news/action-research-classroom-quick-guide

[38] https://miro.com/blog/6-cs-of-education-classroom/

[39] https://www.amle.org/the-4-new-22nd-century-cs-for-education/

[40] https://www.ted.com/

[41] https://allchildrenread.org/

[42] https://www.bbc.co.uk/news/technology-55475433

[43] https://omny.fm/shows/businessbreakfast/stempathy-and-the-science-of-learning-15-02-2017

[44] https://www.tes.com/magazine/article/5-ways-school-leaders-can-put-their-wellbeing-first

[45] https://chemdictionary.org/le-chateliers-principle/

[46] https://www.jfklibrary.org/learn/about-jfk/the-kennedy-family/robert-f-kennedy/robert-f-kennedy-speeches/remarks-at-the-university-of-kansas-march-18-1968

[47] https://simonsinek.com/product/start-with-why/

[48] https://learning.nspcc.org.uk/child-health-development/childhood-trauma-brain-development

[49] https://faculty.washington.edu/kate1/ewExternalFiles/SageOnTheStage.pdf

[50] https://www.simplypsychology.org/Zone-of-Proximal-Development.html

[51] https://allchildrenread.org/

Printed in Great Britain
by Amazon